FORGOTTEN WARRIORS

HISTORY OF KASHMIR AND KASHMIRI PANDITS

RAKESH KOUL

ISBN 979-888546762-9

Contents

About The Book v

1. Frist Queen Of Kashmir Yasovati 1
2. Mihirakula (angry Man Of Kashmir) 7
3. Mauryan Rule(sunrise Of Buddhism In Kashmir) 12
4. Meghavahana 15
5. Kusans In Kashmir (budhism At Its Peak In Kashmir) 17
6. Hun Rule In Kashmir 21
7. Karakota Empire(625-885 Ad) 24
8. Alexander Of Asia Lalitaditya 26
9. Jayapida(grandson Of Lalitaditya) 30
10. Avantivarman(development Man Of Kashmir) 34
11. Queen Sugandha(904-906 Ad) 37
12. Shiva Philosophy Of Kashmir 40
13. Queen Didda(iron Lady Of Kashmir) 45
14. Sangrama Raja 49
15. King Harsha 51
16. Lohara Dynasty 53
17. Kalhana 57
18. The Decline Of Hindu Empire In Kashmir 60
19. Last Queen Of Kashmir Kotrani 62
20. Shah Mir(1339-42) 71
21. Shihab-ud-din 73
22. Sikander The Butshikan 74
23. Lal Ded (1320-1392) 77
24. Ali Shah (1413-30 Ad) 80
25. Sultan Zain -ul-abidin 82
26. Pandit Shriya Bhat 84
27. Nudrishi(sheikh Nur-ud-din) 88

Contents

28. Mir Shama-ud-din Iraqi 91

29. Yusuf Shah Chak 93

30. Haba Khatoon 96

31. Mughal Rule In Kashmir(1580-1750 Ad) 99

32. Afghan Rule In Kashmir (1750-1819) 102

33. Mata Rupa Bhawani(1621-1721) 104

34. Pandit Birbal Dhar 107

35. Arnimal 113

36. The Dogra Rule In Kashmir 115

37. General Zorawar Singh 121

38. Madhav Koul (Unsung Hero Of 1931) 126

39. Pakistan Attack Kashmir (1947) 131

40. Brigadier Rajinder Singh Jamwal 136

41. Major Brown (Occupation Of Gilgit-baltistan) 139

42. Savior Of Kashmir Maqbol Sherwani 142

43. Women Self Defence Corps 144

44. Sheikh Mohammad Abdullah 147

45. Prem Nath Dogra 154

About The Book

This is second book of the series history of Kashmir and Kashmiri Pandits Titled Forgotten Warriors is Indian version of book between the lines it highlights of the history of Kashmir which is already well documented by great scholars of motherland. The main propose of the book is to show the impact the women power in political, literature art and every field in Kashmir. In other parts of ancient India is that woman was deprived from all the types of freedoms. The society was harsh towards the birth of a female child. The rigidness of society clearly reflects where a daughter was considered as source of sufferings and a son savior of the family. In these odds were woman was considered as secondary citizen was not easy for them to be accepted as rulers. To accept women as ruler or advisor to king was a unique and amazing thing that had shaken the foundations of traditional societies, the notion of gender and the womanhood altogether. Woman's involvement in the affairs of the state was almost continuous from the beginning. The most revealing feature of the family life of Kashmir, as seen in these texts is the position of women was no where considered inferior in Kashmir. The picture of society as depicted by Kalhana in his chronicle shows that by his time, woman had emerged from the domestic arena on the political stage. Even during harsh medieval period Kashmir has produced great poetess Lal Ded, Habba Khatoon, Mata Rupa Bhawani and Arnimal .The Nilmata Purana the oldest text of Kashmir shows her to participate in almost all the festivals and religious ceremonies. Kalhana, in his work gives the impression that women received education and were fluent in Sanskrit and Prakit .Aancient history of the Kashmir was first documented in Nilmatpuran and is main source Pandit Kalhana Rajtargni. Authentic sources of Kashmir history are Nilmatpuran (complied 500–600 AD) and Rajatarangini (1150 AD).Kalhana's Rajatarangini (River of Kings) has all the 8000 Sanskrit verses of which were completed by 1150 AD , and chronicles the history of Kashmir's dynasties from Mahabharata times to 12th century .During the reign of Muslim kings in Kashmir, three supplements to Rajatarangini were written by Jonaraja , Srivara, and Prajyabhatta and Suka, which ends with Akbar's conquest of Kashmir in 1586 AD . Kalhana is a renowned name in the world of history, not just because of his work on Kashmir, but also because of what he wrote about the process of historiography and introduces the qualities of a good historian. That is why his Rajatarangini is better than the previous texts. Among his sources were a variety of epigraphic sources relating to royal eulogies, construction of temples, and land grants, coins, monumental remains, family records, local traditions. Kalhana was able to write an unbiased and clear historical writing without any pressure from the kings because he didn't get patronage from any king of his time. His writing was devoid of rhetoric and praise, which was visible in the works of other writers under the patronage of the king's .This past account of the valley, its culture and traditions, rise and fall of various Kingdoms, victory and defeats of the people have been noted carefully, yet critically by the sons of its soil.

CHAPTER ONE

FRIST QUEEN OF KASHMIR YASOVATI

Yasovati (First women ruler of Kashmir)

Kashmir has the distinction of possessing a well recorded history since ancient times. The old Kashmiri texts Rajatararigini of Kalhana and Nilmata Purana, throw light on the status of women in early Kashmir society. Women in Kashmir have enjoyed a more equal status to men than elsewhere and four of them emerged as prominent rulers. In Kalhana's Rajatarangini three famous women rulers have been mentioned and they were Yasovati of Gonda dynasty, Sugandha (904-906 AD) of the Utpala dynasty and Didda (980/1-1003 AD) of Viradeva dynasty. The fourth queen and the last queen who ruled Kashmir was Kota Rani. But the first queen ruler of Kashmir Yasovati who legalized the woman rule in Kashmir and laid its foundation. In other parts of ancient India is that woman was deprived from all the types of freedoms. The society was harsh towards the birth of a female child. The rigidness of society clearly reflects where a daughter was considered as source of sufferings and a son savior of the family. In these odds were woman was considered as secondary citizen was not easy for them to be accepted as rulers. To accept women as ruler or advisor to king was a unique and amazing thing that had shaken the foundations of traditional societies, the notion of gender and the womanhood altogether. Woman's involvement in the affairs of the state was almost continuous from the beginning. The most revealing feature of the family life of Kashmir, as seen in these texts is the position of women was no where considered inferior in Kashmir. The picture of society as depicted by Kalhana in his chronicle shows that by his time, woman had emerged from the domestic arena on the political stage. The Nilmata Purana the oldest text of Kashmir shows her to participate in almost all the festivals and religious ceremonies. Kalhana, in his work gives the impression that women, of at least the upper classes, received education and were fluent in Sanskrit and Prakit (Now forgotten language currently there is no independent degree in Prakrit, but it is offered as a subsidiary language for the BA in Sanskrit. Students can still study Prakrit language and literature, as well as the doctrine and early histories of Jainism. Several Prakrits have been identified. Pali, the language the Buddha preached in and Ardhamagadhi, which was Mahavira's tongue are both Prakrits with their larger philosophy of reaching out to the masses. Indeed, much of the Buddhist and Jain religious corpus are in these tongues. Ashoka had his edicts inscribed in Prakrit, again deliberately, to ensure that people understood his message. These Prakrits are among the oldest that are known. Around the time of Ashoka, or perhaps a little later, it appears that Pali was taken to Sri Lanka by Buddhist monks and later evolved into modern day Sinhalese). From the picture which Kalhana has depicted in his chronicle, it becomes clear that women of this period were not only receiving education of a general nature but in diplomacy and statecraft too. They had moreover, to learn botany, painting, needlework, woodwork, clay-modeling, cookery and receive practical training in instrumental music, singing and dancing. No wonder, we find the women of Kashmir as active as men in of Public duties. We find for instance, women seated along with other officials and ministers in the court have examples of heroism displayed by queen Didda and later by Kota Rani.

Gonanda Dynasty

Gonanda I (3238-3188 BC) was relative of Magadha ruler Jarasandha. He was killed by Krishna's elder brother Balarama. His son Damodara I was killed by Krishna and his army. Later Krishna made his wife Yasovati as temporary ruler for 6 months, who was succeeded by her son Gonanda II. Gonanda II was Killed in a battle with Parikshit (grandson of Arjuna), king of Hastinapura in 3083 BCE.As Gonanda II has no heir at time of death, Parikshit took over the kingdom of Kashmir, incorporated it into his empire and handed it over to Harnadeva, who was from his family. From Harnadeva, Pandava dynasty kings ruled over Kashmir for 1331 years from 3083-1752 BCE.Gonanda-II had 7 wives. Gonanda-II's mother Yasovati, along with her pregnant elder daughter-in-law Sudhalahari, ran away and took shelter at her maternal kingdom of Videha. Gonanda dynasty heir was raised there but for many generations, they could not re-capture their Kashmir Kingdom. Their descendants survived in multiple regions through many years but never had the courage or strength to attack heirs of Harnadeva. But they were raised with the thought that they belonged to Gonanda Dynasty. After 1331 years, Lava gathered enough army and killed Bhagavanta, the last descendant of Harnadeva (relative of Pandavas) and restarted Gonanda dynasty rule.

After 1331 years, Lava gathered enough army and killed Bhagavanta, the last descendant of Harnadeva (relative of Pandavas) and restarted Gonanda dynasty rule. But Gonanda dynasty lost power again during the tenure of Andh Yudhishtira (He was called Andh Yudhishtira by the people, because of his having small eyes. In fact he was not blind.). In whose period, the affairs of the country soon fell in to disorder. His wicked councilors made the rulers of neighboring countries eager to seize the kingdom finally; he was made to leave the kingdom. He was called the blind because of his small eyes. In later years of his reign, he started patronizing unwise persons, and the wise courtiers deserted him. He was deposed by rebellious ministers, and granted asylum by a neighboring king. His descendant Meghavahana later restored the dynasty's rule. Partapaditya was made king of by the ministers of who had rebelled against the king Andh Yudhishtira. After

Partapaditya Jalauka son of Ashoka the great established the direct rule of Mauryan Empire in Kashmir

Son of Great grandson of the Andh Yudhishtira Meghavahana reestablished Gonanda Dynasty again in the Kashmir. It was Gonanda who ruled most of the time in Kashmir they were thrown out of power many time but they kept the faith and hope and returned back. Meghavahana son was Gopaditya a great grandson of Andh Yudhishtira who had been living in exile at the court of the king of Gandhara. Meghavahana, he is supposed to have taken possession of the throne of his forefathers at the invitation of the Kashmiri Ministers

Yasovati as Ruler

Yasovati was first recorded female ruler of ancient Kashmir. It was Krishna, the descendant of Yadavas, who had installed the king's wife on the throne .Kalhana refers that advisers at that time were grumbling that a woman had been crowned queen. Some of the disloyal ministers of the state were filled with greed and attempt to capture the throne. Although Yasovati herself has a shadowy presence, the rule of woman is justified by lord Krishna's injunction that all occupants of the throne are portions of Shiva and, therefore, need to be obeyed, thereby providing a strong divine sanction to male and female ruler-ship in Kashmir. It proved fruitful for the women of Kashmir, because in other regions religious texts and other literally source were used to curb the freedom of woman and while as in Kashmir texts were referred to give free hand to woman in ruler-ship. The advisers, who initially challenged the women rule in Kashmir because of their greed and changed their view; sincerely started obeying the queen as ruler. First king of mentioned Nilmatpuran as well in Kalhana's Rajtargni is Gonanda1.The Nilmatpuran opens with Janamejaya's enquiry from Vaisampayana as to why the king of Kashmir did not participate in the war of the Mahabharata although his kingdom was not less important than any other in the country. Vaisampayana states that some time before the Mahabharata war was fought, king Gonanda of Kashmir had been invited by his relative Jarasandha to help him in a war against the yadavas. Gonanda complied with his request and was killed the battle field by Lord Krishna's brother Balarama. In order to avenge his father's death, Gonanda's son Damodara went to Gandhara to fight with lord Krishna who had gone there to attend a Svayamvara. Krishna killed Damodara in the fight but taking into consideration the high sanctity of Kashmir he crowned his pregnant widow Yasovati. Damodara Posthumous son Bala Gonanda was a minor at the time of the Great War, so he did not join either the Kauravas or the Pandavas. It was prior to Mahabharata war the king of Kashmir Gonanda I was invited by his relative Jarasandha, king of Magadha to help him in war against the Yadavas. On the invitation for help in the war, the king of Kashmir with huge forces marched towards the battle field on the banks of river Yamuna. The king of Kashmir fought bravely in the battle field, and got injured while fighting. Finally the king of Kashmir lost his life while fighting with the enemies of his relative's .Kalhana had high praises for the king of Kashmir, Gonanda I, who lost his life in battlefield. He further refers that this great hero was succeed by his son Damodara I. The new king Damodara I was filled with ideas of revenge for his father's death. He was waiting eagerly to attack his father's killers. It was on occasion of Svayamvara the king attacked Krishna at Gandhara on the banks of Indus. The king fought bravely but at the end lost his life. It was after the death of king Damodara I Kashmir witnessed the woman rule for the first time. After the death of king Damodara I, who left no heir behind and his pregnant wife Yasovati was installed on throne of Kashmir. Yasovati is First recorded female ruler of ancient Kashmir. It proved fruitful for the women of Kashmir, because in other regions religious texts and other literally source were used to curb the freedom of woman and while as in Kashmir texts were referred to give free hand to woman in ruler-ship. Unfortunately a detailed description of Yasovati reign is not available. Even though the rule of queen was not given much importance but she laid the foundation stone of women rule in Kashmir. In Rajtarangini that the Kalhana only dedicated five verses to the queen .She was the first who legalized the women rule in Kashmir. As the sovereign queen ruling in her own right or as a regent administering the country on behalf of her son, Yasovati proved a successful and popular ruler who fully understands her duties and efficiently discharged the responsibilities entrusted to her care. The queen ruler justified the women rule and emerged a challenge to the male dominated succession. After the queen ascension to the throne it bears that woman even can take the charge of administration if the king died without male heir or left infant behind. This was a counter attack to those law givers and other literally source that in succession only male heirs can possess the hereditary rights of ruler-ship. From the reign of queen we can say that the law givers and other literally sources whose writings helped in the easy subjugation women, lost authority in the region of Kashmir or we can say find no space in this land. But her role in the history of Kashmir, especially helping the women to live standard life can't be denied. The queen acquired such a position in the history of Kashmir that became a source of reference for the royal and non-royal ladies. After her it became notion in the Kashmir that woman can rule over the subjects clearly seen in the emergence of women rulers like, queen Sugandha, Didda and Kota Rani. The queen became the forerunner of other queen rulers of Kashmir. Her reign was short but makes the path of women ruler-ship easy and acceptable.

CHAPTER TWO

MIHIRAKULA (ANGRY MAN OF KASHMIR)

Mihirakula (angry man of Kashmir)

Mihirakula was only son of Vasukula and he developed a passion for war and had physical training since childhood. Vasukula understood intentions of his son, kept him under house arrest for 10 days and starved to death. During these 10 days, Mihirakula slowly took over the administration in 704 BC. After death of his father, he tried to coronate himself as king, but Pandits objected to this, saying that only a married man has rights to get coronate as king. Mihirakula continued to rule without official coronation ceremony and launched invasions on neighboring kingdoms. During one of his attacks, he sent a message to Gandhara King (modern day Kandahar in Afghanistan) to chose between surrender and war. One night, Gandhara princess Kalyanavati, dressed as a male soldier, came to Mihirakula and offered her hand in marriage as a compromise. Mihirakula married her and got officially coronated as king of Kashmir.

Sadistic nature of Mihirakula

The king enforced law and order by strict punishments. Every evening he used to visit the jail where prisoners are kept and punishments were like, smashing joint bones with sharp iron rods and then piercing those bleeding joints, peeling off the skin or removing organs while keeping the prisoner alive. King used to gain pleasure by listening to their screams. He felt happier while women screamed with pain. His father-in-law had no sons, so he got involved and killed all those who revolted and convinced Gandhara king to adopt one of his relative's sons Neelanka. During this process, he captured lakhs of men who revolted against king. He also captured those who helped Mlecchas from neighboring countries. Women who committed adultery with Mlecchas were also captured and brought to Kashmir, where they were cruelly punished. He used to worship Betala, Yama but never felt satisfied with all the mass murders. Mihirakula Elephant on Mountain Cliff One night, his deity appeared in dream and said that he will get to know source for more satisfaction by next morning Mihirakula woke up in morning by hearing a big scream that came from nearby mountains. Enquiry, he gets to know that an elephant from army, slipped along with mountain cliff rock during routine military exercise and died. While slipping off the cliff, the elephant screamed along with Mahout (elephant trainer) and king realized the source of his satisfaction .King ordered that the cliff rock which fell along with elephant, should be pulled up and reinstated on mountain. It took one full day to achieve it and in this process many soldiers died. From next morning, king ordered that every morning before sunrise, Mahouts will take elephants onto the cliff and slip off. Every morning king used to wake up with sounds of elephants screaming with fear of death. Those dead bodies were recovered and cremated each day. There were Mahouts who revolted against this process, but they were thrown off the mountain peak. Elephant killing process went on for 150 days and ultimately Mihirakula felt satisfied and stopped it.

Mihirakula murdered Women

While he was diverting the river Chandrakulya, a rock in midstream which was impossible to remove, caused obstruction. Then to the king who had practiced penance, his deity spoke in a dream that, a mighty Yaksa who is a Brahmachari resides here in the rock. Only a chaste woman (Pativrata, who never committed adultery in her life), should touch the rock and can move it. The following day, king ordered every married woman in nearby village to touch the rock .Women kept coming but failed to move it .At last king asked his wife Kalyanavati to touch it. She too tried but failed. Upon witnessing failure of queen, other women did not dare to attempt. At last, a washerwoman named Chandravati came forward and moved with rock. She was offered 10000 gold coins and many gifts.10 days later, King ordered mass murders of all the village women who failed to move the rock. All those women were made to stand on the river bank and soldiers chopped their heads off. Those who tried to run away were caught and killed. The entire place was filled with dead bodies of women. Queen came to know about this and objected. Remaining women were sent off with their husbands. Next day she asked king to fight with her but king, who already coronated his son Baka, jumped into a fire pit and committed suicide. He felt guilty for killing other women, except his wife. Kalyanavati too committed suicide by stabbing herself immediately.

Attack on Sinhala King (Sri Lanka)

After marriage, Mihirakula reduced violence and remained in his capital for some time. One day, he saw his wife Kalyanavati wearing an upper cloth made of a silk. The cloth was a special type of weave (similar to Barleycorn weave, in Sanskrit: Yamusha Deva) with golden foot prints on it. King noticed that those gold foot prints were embroidered on breasts part of the blouse. He enquired about origin of this cloth and understood that they were weaved in Sinhala Kingdom (Sri Lanka) and sold in other kingdoms. Those foot prints were of Sinhala King. Mihirakula Queen Blouse from Sinhala turned Silent Mihirakula violent and launched an attack on Sinhala. He 3Huge army travelled south and reached Rameswaram. From there, thousands of ships, boats were used to reach Sinhala (Lanka) Island. Sinhala army had no time to understand that they were under an attack and before they could know the reason, Mihirakula killed all soldiers guarding the gates. He smashed open the doors of fort and captured Sinhala King. He bought his wife's blouse with those footprints and upon confirming that they belonged to Sinhala King, he killed him by squeezing his neck. Mihirakula stayed in Sinhala for one month and coronated one of the dead king's descendant. He installed Kala Bhairava idol in Sinhala capital and every day offered garland made of 108 skulls, which belonged to Sinhala soldiers. Buddhism established in Lanka by Asoka was followed by many during this attack. Mihirakula killed large number of them. Meanwhile, Tamil, Karnataka, Chera (Kerala) kings sent their armies to help Sinhala King. Their boats were turned upside down in sea by Kashmir army. Mihirakula brought all the Yamusha Deva cloth with foot prints from entire Sinhala and burnt it. Later he took the remaining cloth which had no footprints with him back to Kashmir. During his return journey, he attacked and defeated those kings who tried to help Sinhala king. His army burnt villages, killed uncountable men and women. Wells were dried of water but filled with blood. He captured lakhs of soldiers and reached Kashmir along with tons of Yamusha Deva cloth and dead body of Sinhala King. By that time, Kalyanavati delivered a male child. He was later named Baka. Mihirakula brother-in-law, who was Gandhara king's adopted son, used to call him Bakasura for his violent nature of killing multiple people each day. To remember this nick name, Mihirakula named his son as Baka, but he turned out to be a soft natured person after growing up. Mihirakula said to his Queen Kings of Bharat could not understand the insult of this person's footprints being on breasts of their wives. But, similar to Sri Rama, who attacked Lanka to avenge his wife's kidnap; i too attacked Sinhala and brought this king's dead body to show you. Saying this, he threw that foot printed blouse on Sinhala king's dead body and burnt him. He distributed all the Yamusha Deva cloth among his men and asked it to be sent to all kingdoms in Bharat Varsha. After the death of Mihirakula, his son Baka was crowned by the subjects. He built a Shiva temple for Baka and ruled the country for sixty three years. A virtuous king, he was seduced and killed by a woman named Vatta, along with several of his sons and grandsons. Kshitinanda The only surviving child of Baka, Vasunanda, Nara II, Aksha and Gopaditya became kings in succession after him. His son Gokarna ruled for about fifty eight years. He was followed by Narendraditya and then by Andh Yudhishtira (He was called Andh Yudhishtira by the people, because of his having small eyes. In fact he was not blind.). In whose period, the affairs of the country soon fell in to disorder. His wicked councilors made the rulers of neighboring countries eager to seize the kingdom finally; he was made to leave the kingdom. He was called the blind because of his small eyes. In later years of his reign, he started patronizing unwise persons, and the wise courtiers deserted him. He was deposed by rebellious ministers, and granted asylum by a neighboring king. His descendant Meghavahana later restored the dynasty's rule. Partapaditya was made king of by the ministers of who had rebelled against the king Andh Yudhishtira. After Partapaditya Jalauka son of Ashoka the great established the direct rule of Mauryan Empire in Kashmir

CHAPTER THREE

MAURYAN RULE(Sunrise of Buddhism in Kashmir)

(Ashoka the great)

Mauryan rule (Sunrise of Buddhism in Kashmir)

The direct rule of the Mauryan in Kashmir was established the Jalauka son of Ashoka the great after the death Partapaditya of established the direct rule of Mauryan Empire in Kashmir. Jalauka was devoted to the worship of the Hindu god Shiva and the Divine Mothers, in whose honor he and his queen, Isana-devi, erected many temples in places which can be identified.

Even though It was Ashoka who came into contact with Kashmir in his early life that but he had not established direct rule in Kashmir. Kalhana's reference to Asoka's building in Kashmir valley indicates that his stay in Kashmir was quite long. Chandragupta's successor Bindusara had appointed him as the Governor of Kashmir and Gandhara so it t can be inferred that he paid regular visits to the beautiful valley when he became the emperor of Magadha Empire. Asoka's reign was marked by great building activity and spread of Buddhism. It was the Ashoka who laid foundation of town Srinagari, three miles above the modern city of Srinagar. It had ninety six thousand dwelling houses splendid with prosperity the important event concerned with Asoka's reign was the spread of Buddhism in Kashmir. Buddhism was an important part of the classical Kashmiri culture, as is reflected in the Nilmata Purana and Kalhana's Rajatarangini. Buddhism but it becomes dominant in Kashmir in the time of Emperor Ashoka, although it was widespread there long before his time, enjoying the patronage not only of Buddhist rulers but of Hindu rulers too. From Kashmir, it spread to the neighboring Ladhak, Tibet and China. Accounts of patronage of Buddhism by the rulers of Kashmir are found in the Rajatarangini and also in the accounts.

According to some Buddhist writers including Taranatha, the Buddhist preacher Madhyantika introduced saffron cultivation into Kashmir. Buddhism and Shaivism flourished side by side in Kashmir during Asoka's time and received the Emperor's patronage in equal measure. Kalhana notes that Ashoka built two Shiva temples at Vijayeshvara (Bijbehara), and ordered several others renovated. In Vitastatra (Vethavutur) and at Shuskaletra (Hukhalitar) he built a number of Viharas and stupas.

Buddhism suffered a temporary eclipse during the reign of Asoka's successors Jalauka .Kalhana, asserted that a large number of Buddhist scholars were vanquished in debates with Jalauka guru Avadhuta, and hence traditional observances were slowly revived. Later, however, Jalauka created a big Vihara, the Krityashrama vihara in the vicinity of Varahamula (Baramulla)

In the age of Ashoka when Buddhism was carried to the valley, the text and literature of the new religion were written in Sanskrit, in contrast to those written in Pali in the rest of India. With the development of Mahayana the entire Buddhism literature was composed in the Sanskrit language and it was perhaps because of this that Sanskrit was diffused in central Asia by the numerous Buddhist missionaries from Kashmir. In recent years a large number of Sanskrit Buddhist manuscript ever discovered in India has come from Gilgit in Kashmir.

Not only did the students from the rest of India come to the valley for higher studies, but we find pilgrims and scholars from central Asia and china coming to Kashmir to study Sanskrit texts. Hsuen Tsiang spent two years in the valley studying Buddhist texts in Sanskrit and so did the earlier scholar spent years in Kashmir .In the age of Ashoka, Sanskrit was written both on the kharosthi and the brahmi script. In Kashmir, the scholars developed a script of their own the Sarada which though differing from the Devanagri details, follows it in its essentials. In the 9th century AD the Tibetans who had no script for their language adopted the Sarada script of Kashmir.Budhism flourished kings such as Jalouk, Hushka, Jushka followed by the great King Kanishka. The last three kings including Kanishka belonged to the famous Kusana royal dynasty. This glorious Buddhist period in Kashmir was known as the Golden Age of Kashmir. By the latter part of the 1st century, during the reign of Emperor Kanishka, Kashmir became the foremost centre of Mahayana Buddhism. The introduction of Buddhism to Kashmir is of great historic importance because it was from Kashmir that Buddhism spread to the Himalayan region and beyond, to Qandahar, Kabul, Bactria and Tibet. Kashmir also played an important role in spread of Buddhism to Central Asia and eventually China

CHAPTER FOUR

MEGHAVAHANA

(Meghavahana)

Meghavahana (25-59 AD)

Great grandson of the Andh Yudhishtira Meghavahana reestablished Gonanda Dynasty again in the Kashmir. It was Gonanda who ruled most of the time in Kashmir they were thrown out of power many time but they kept the faith and hope and returned back. Meghavahana son was Gopaditya a great grandson of Andh Yudhishtira who had been living in exile at the court of the king of Gandhara. Meghavahana, who is supposed to have taken possession of the throne of his forefathers at the invitation of the Kashmiri ministers, is described as a strong but pious ruler. He married Amritaprabha, daughter of the king Bala Varman of Kamarupa. His son and successor is Sresthasena. But during the time Meghavahana from was installed in the throne by the subjects Buddhism was at rise even the Gonanda's had accepted. This king prohibited the killing of living beings in his country and helped the butchers and others in finding other means of livelihood. Bhutabali in the sacrifices was by an effigy made of ghee, in the shape of the animal to be sacrificed. He had many wives and all were associated with building Viharas for Bhikshus. This king went forth for the conquest of the world not with sword but with friendship and humanity so that he could impose upon the other kings his prohibition against the killing of living beings. He then proceeds to Lanka on an expedition and makes friends with king Vasabha. To seek forgiveness from king of Lanka at that Vasabha for the crimes committed by his predecessor king Mihirakula in the Lanka .King Vasabha born to a family of a clan named Lambakanna spent his childhood in a village in the North of the country working for his uncle who was a general in the king's army. Having eventually raised an army, Vasabha led a rebellion against the king, and subsequently seized the throne in 67 AD after killing Subharaja and his uncle. He ruled for 44 years, until his death in 111 AD. His accession to the throne marked the beginning of a new dynasty of rulers, known as the First Lambakanna Dynasty after the name of his clan. He returned to Varuna his parasol, which was taken away from him by the father-in-law of his father and was praised by Varuna for abstention from killing beings as though as a prayaschitta for the sin committed by his predecessor Mihirakula.

CHAPTER FIVE

KUSANS IN KASHMIR (BUDHISM AT ITS PEAK IN KASHMIR)

(KANSHIKA)

Kanishka 2nd century (120-144 AD)

Kanishka was a tolerant king, and his coins show that he honored the Zoroastrian, Greek, and Brahmnaical deities as well as the Buddha. During his reign, contacts with the Roman Empire via the Silk Road led to a significant increase in trade and the exchange of ideas; perhaps the most remarkable example of the fusion of Eastern and Western influences in his reign was the Gandhara School of art, in which Classical Greco-Roman lines are seen in images of the Buddha. His capital was Peshawar were a Kanishka Stupa, once a marvel of India, being the tallest building even in 7th century. Hieun Tsang, who visited Kashmir in the early 7th century A.D. found local traditions regarding Kanishka rule still fully alive in the Valley. And it appeared so true to the Chinese pilgrim that he faithfully recorded them in his travel account, particularly the holding of fourth great Buddhist Council by Kanishka. The continued existence of a place called Kanishkapur in district Baramulla, described as a foundation of Kanishka, till present times, is a living him from his father which he certainly preserved. The variety of his coins in gold and copper are equally suggestive of the peace and prosperity in his time. Huvishka's name figures among the three Kusana rulers mentioned by Rajatarangini, to have ruled Kashmir. He also credits him for having built a town Hushkapura (Huvishkapura) after his name. The town survives in modem Ushkur, a village about three kilometers to the southeast of Baramulla on the left bank of Vitasta (Jhelum). He also attributes to him and the other two Kusana rulers the construction of stupas and matha at Suskaletra. Huvishka's rule in Kashmir is also corroborated by his gold coin found by chance somewhere in the valley. Like his father (Kanishka), Huvishka's coins also portrayed the divinities drawn from different Pantheons, although in the Indian environment the tendency seems more towards the depiction of new Brahmnaical deities. This undoubtedly alludes to syncretism religious system promoted by Kanishka and his successors. As a patron of Buddhism, Kanishka is chiefly noted for having convened the fourth great Buddhist council in Kashmir, which marked the beginnings of Mahayana Buddhism. At the council, according to Chinese sources, authorized commentaries on the Buddhist canon were prepared and engraved on copper plates. These texts have survived only in Chinese translations and adaptations.

Evidently, during the period of Kanishka Kashmir attained unprecedented prosperity. This is evident from the Kushan art treasures with Buddhist themes found in different nooks of the valley. Significantly enough Rajatarangini of Kalhana makes a special mention of him as besides clubbing the building activities of the three Kusana rulers (Kanishka, Jushka and Huska) and the efflorescence of Buddhism during their rule, Rajtarangni writes exceptionally about Juska .That wise king Juska, who built Juskapura with its Vihara, was also the founder of Jayasvamipura.As a matter of fact Kushan occupation of Kashmir paved the way for the influx of a culture which was an amalgam of Chinese, Central Asian, Iranian, Greek and Indian civilizations, which Far reaching promoted Kashmir's technology, economy and culture besides giving it a cosmopolitan character. More importantly, Kashmir got integrated with the world market by giving the Kashmiri trader access to Silk Route which was under the control of the Kushans. That trade with the outside world was greatly promoted under the Kushans is substantiated by hoards of coins found on the trade routes between Kashmir and china (Silk route)

CHAPTER SIX

HUN RULE IN KASHMIR

(TORAMANA)

Hun rule in Kashmir (493 to 597)

The Huns were nomadic warriors who terrorized much of Europe and the Roman Empire in the 4th and 5th centuries A.D. They were impressive horsemen best known for their astounding military achievements. The Huns acquired a reputation for being ruthless, indomitable savages. Huns were in fact a very problematic people. They are problematic in that everything from their origins, their religion, their customs, names, tribal affiliations etc are all under dispute. This is coupled with the obvious ability of these people to fully integrate with the conquered regions .adopting religions, customs, cities and even states as their homes. They shunned their previous nomadic lives and slowly become so much a part of the fabric of society .Huns specifically in Gandhara, as that of fire worship fire worship or sun worship, although not unusual in that time of history, still allows us to connect the Huns with an early Zoroastrian religion later integrated into Hinduism as well.

The first Hun king of any importance was Toramana, who ruled northern India as far as Madhya Pradesh in central India. Toramana's son Toramana 2 appears to have been more of the Hun as pictured by tradition. The Toramana 2 was nicked named by the Buddhists monks as Mihirakula due to cruel nature which was even harsher the ancient Gonanda king Mihirakula (Angry man of Kashmir). Although he is considered a great ruler in terms of military conquests for the Huns .Empire, Mihirakula is not remembered the same way his father was. He is thought to have been a harsh and cruel ruler who was not loved at all by his subjects, and is considered the reason why the Huna name was feared and eventually opposed in the subcontinent by local rulers. Toramana 2 (Mihirakula) destroyed Buddhist sites, ruined monasteries. Yasovarman, about 532 AD, reversed Mihirakula campaign and started the end of Mihirakula era. Mihirakula issued coins, like the Kushan era kings, showing Shiva, which suggests that he may also have patronized Shaivism. Mihirakula had conquered Kashmir first, then Gandhara. He is also mentioned as attempting to conquer central and eastern India, but was defeated by Yasovarman and the Gupta king Narasimhagupta (Baladitya). He persecuted the Buddhists and strictly followed Shivite Hinduism. He even built a temple in Kashmir while residing there for the worship of Shiva. His troops were said to have destroyed 1400 monasteries in central Gandhara, Kashmir and the Northwestern Subcontinent, the areas where he had the most solid rule. Remoter areas such as Mardan and Swat were spared as they were not easily accessible and were consequently left a certain degree of autonomy. Strangely enough before his persecution he was actually interested in the religion. After his defeat in 533 CE by Yasodharman in the West, Mihirakula tried to consolidate his power in the East of his Empire around Patna, but was defeated by the king Baladitya there, who did not kill Mihirakula, who then withdrew to Kashmir. He eventually ascended the Kashmiri throne through guile and deceit but did not manage to keep power for too long, dying in 533 CE of disease. While in Kashmir, he reformed his forces and attacked the Gandhara region again, killing the entire royal family there and burning Buddhist temples and stupas. He also massacred half the people there who were of Buddhist faith after that his half brother and son of Toramana became the he had been completed absorbed in the rich culture of the Kashmir at that time. He was complete opposite to his half brother Toramana 2 (Mihirakula) and father Toramana .He was the younger son of Toramana by another wife, and was vehemently opposed by his half-brother Mihirakula, for which reason he was hidden away after Toramana died and remained in the North of India as a pilgrim until the death of his brother. Then he ascended the Kashmiri throne in either 533 or 537 CE at the age of 25. He is known to have ruled for 60 years up until 597 CE and was considered to be a strong and loyal ally who was accepted by his subjects, unlike his predecessor. He is also considered to have founded Srinagar in Kashmir and raised a temple near the city for the worship of Shiva. He founded the Pravarsenapura or Pravarapura (Modern Srinagar) around Hari Parbat. He plans as Shiva temple at Pravarapura, but miraculously a Vishnu image appears at the place, he names it Jayasvamin temple after the architect of the temple.

CHAPTER SEVEN

KARAKOTA EMPIRE(625-885 AD)

Karakota Empire (625 - 885 AD)

Karakota Empire (625 - 885 AD) was a major power in the Indian subcontinent during 7th and 8th century. It was founded by Durlabhavardhana. The dynasty marked the rise of Kashmir as a power in Northern India. Lalitaditya Muktapida, the dynasty's strongest ruler captured parts of Central Asia, Afghanistan and Punjab with Chinese help. The strongest ruler of the dynasty was Lalitaditya. Some of the main conquests he made were up to Bengal that made Kashmir the most powerful kingdom after the time of The Guptas. The Martand temple in the Anantnag district of today's Kashmir preserves the memory of King Lalitaditya. These details are described in the Rajtarangini of Kalhana. During his reign, he encouraged the developments in the fields of art and architecture. His capital Parihaspura had four temples at the time, tons of gold, silver, copper and brass were used to decorate the temples. There are many sculptors of Buddha's were excavated, also the rule experienced the widespread of Hinduism and Buddhism. Karakota rule was at its peak during the reign of Lalitaditya, but unfortunately the dynasty was preceded by weak rulers which were not capable to unite the scattering kingdom after the death of Lalitaditya. They lost the glory of the kingdom and the dynasty was replaced by Utpala Dynasty. He establishing the Utpala dynasty and ending the rule of Karakota dynasty in 855 AD

It is the Karakota dynasty that has given Kashmir the greatest ruler Lalitaditya Muktapida (724- 761 A. D.). He is undoubtedly the Alexander of India. He was filled with an unquenchable thirst of world conquest. He invaded and conquered many countries in Asia and India. The Punjab, Kanauj, Tibet, Ladhak, Badakhshan, Iran, Bihar, Gauda (Bengal) Kalinga

(Orissa), South India, Gujarat, Malwa, Marwar and Sindh were all conquered by him. It was he, who finally broke the power of Arabs in Sindh. All these unbroken victories created a feeling of pride among the people here and his victories came to be celebrated in a big way. Kalhan who wrote his famous chronicle (Rajatarangini) nearly four hundred years after the death of Lalitaditya, records that even in his time the victories of the great victor were being celebrated throughout the valley. Alberuni, who accompanied Mahmud Ghazanavi in his Indian Campaigns, specifically mentions in his book (Tahqiq-i-Hind) that Kashmiri observed second of Chaitra, as the day of victory. Lalitaditya was equally a great builder and he built his capital near the sacred shrine of Khir-Bhawani, and gave it the name of Parihaspura (city of pleasure). Throughout the valley, he built very fine and massive temples, out of which the world famous sun temple (Martand) built on Mattan Karewa, reminds us about the grandeur and splendor of the times when their builder ruled the state. The extensive ruins of his capital city Parihaspura, speak of his activities in the field of art and architecture. After his death, it is mostly the weak rulers except his grandson Jayapida, who ruled the valley. Both Lalitaditya and Jayapida were great patrons of learning and extended their patronage to Bhavabhuti, Vakpatrija, Udhata Bhata, Damodhar Gupta, Manoratha, Sankhdanta and Samadhimat etc. The history of Karakota dynasty after Jayapida is a sad story of decline. All the conquered territories regained their independence, and the sovereignty of the ruler of Kashmir came to be confined to Vitasta basin. The economic ruin was hastened by the extravagant habits of both the rulers and the ministers. In the words of Kalhan the ministers and the grandees carried-off the revenues of the country, feasted in mutual jealousy on the master less kingdom, like wolves on a dead buffalo in a desert. In spite of all this the Karakota rule on the whole has been considered as the glorious and remarkable periods of ancient Kashmir. It was round about in 855-56 A. D. that Karakota rule ended, and a new Utpal Dynasty assumed power in Kashmir.

CHAPTER EIGHT

ALEXANDER OF ASIA LALITADITYA

Alexander of Asia Lalitaditya (724-760)

Lalitaditya called the Alexander of Asia was greatest king ever produced by the continent but still our historians have not paid much attention to him

Lalitaditya Conquered

Dardistan or Darad Desha: Modern day Northern Pakistan and parts of north-eastern Afghanistan, Turkestan, Modern day Turkmenistan, Kazakhstan, Uzbekistan, Kyrgyzstan & Xinjiang,Kingdoms of Kucha &Turfan Modern day East China, He also Defeated & routed The Arab Caliphate Army in 730 AD

One has only to leaf through the pages of our ancient history to be reminded of some of the greatest conquerors of the bygone times. There have been illustrious rulers who were both great builders as well as conquerors. One of them Lalitaditya-Muktapida of Karakota dynasty who ruled Kashmir from 724 to 760 AD was greatest king ever. Karakota dynasty had come to rule Kashmir after Baladitya, the last King of the passed away. Durlabhavardhana was Baladitya son in law and after his death was established on the throne of Kashmir. He was followed by his son Partapaditya-II who had three sons, Candrapida, Tarapida, and Muktapida, also known as Vajraditya, Udayaditya, and Lalitaditya. Candrapida and Tarapida ruled for 8 years and 4 years respectively. Lalitaditya-Muktapida was the youngest son of Partapaditya-II and followed Tarapida. Kalhan describes Lalitaditya as a very strong ruler, who asserted his power far beyond Kashmir and the adjacent territories. He is represented as a great conqueror, whose reign was mostly passed in expeditions abroad. The numerous foreign expeditions of Lalitaditya and his ultimate disappearance on one of these forays towards north reminds one of the Greek Conqueror, Alexander the Great who was of a similar disposition and in that respect Lalitaditya may be called Kashmir's Alexander. The descriptions of his foreign expeditions have a mixture of historical and legendary details. His first enterprise was directed against Yasovarman, the ruler of Kanyakubja or Kanauj. After the defeat of Yasovarman, the King is supposed to have triumphantly marched round whole of India, from Bengal and Orissa in the east to Kathiawar and Kambojas (Afghanistan) in the west. After defeating Yasovarman, Lalitaditya is supposed to have invaded and subdued Tukharas, a nation in the northern region. The country of Tukharas is undoubtedly the Tokharistan of the Muslim period comprising Badakhshan. These were definitely belonging to a family of Turkish origin ruling Kabul Valley and Gandhara. The famous Chinese pilgrim to Kashmir, Ou-kong mentions that there were close relations between contemporary Kashmir and Turkish tribes. Turkish prince Cankuna was in the court of Lalitaditya. Kalhana also mentions that Kashmir at that time used to celebrate annually on a certain day a festival to commemorate the victory which their King

Muktapida had won over Turks. Next in the list of conquests come the Tibetans. The Annals of Tang dynasty of China know Lalitaditya-Muktapida under the name of Mu-to-pi, as the King of Kashmir who sent an embassy to the Chinese court during the reign of Emperor Hiuen-tsung (AD 713-755). The main purpose of the embassy had been to seek alliance of the Chinese rulers against Tibet. Ambassador U-li- to whom Mu-to-pi had sent to the imperial court distinctly claimed for his master repeated victories over Tibetans. The auxiliary Chinese force of two hundred thousand men which the Kashmir King invited to his country and for which he proposed to establish a camp on the shores of Mahapadma or Volur Lake, was meant for further operations against the common foe. There is evidence that the Tibetans had established a powerful empire at that time and had threatened both Kashmir as well as China. As there is no evidence of any Tibetans invasion of Kashmir, one must assume that Lalitaditya expeditions towards north were real and lasting and checked the Tibetan march towards Kashmir. Lalitaditya had also subdued Kashmir's immediate northern neighbors', the Dards. The Dard tribes have from very early times to the present day inhabited the mountain territories immediately adjoining Kashmir to the north and north-west. The very safety of the valley has many times necessitated expeditions against these areas. Apart from these numerous conquests and foreign expeditions, Lalitaditya had been a builder of renown. Numerous shrines and sacred images were erected during his time. The ruins of the splendid Sun Temple of Martanda are still the most striking object of ancient Hindu architecture in the Valley. The location of the Temple itself is very prominent. The ruins of the Temple are even at present a great attraction for tourists especially from Europe. Kalhan mentions about the town of Martanda near the Temple which was swelling with grapes. There is no trace of the town now. The most important proof of the scale and extent of the building operations of Lalitaditya are the ruins of Parihaspura which he built as his new capital. The plateau where Lalitaditya built his capital is now known as Parspor Udar. It rises south-east of Shadipur between the marshes of Panznor and Hartrath. Its length is about two miles and width is about a mile. There are ruins of numerous temples, vihara, and other structures here. Kalhan says that Lalitaditya had once under the influence of liquor ordered that the city of Srinagar (Pravarapura) be set on fire if it was thought by people to be better than his capital Parihaspura. His ministers set fire to some bundles of hay and informed him that they had set Srinagar on fire. In the morning, King was very much tormented that he had burned down Srinagar and was relieved only after he was told that the burning was only a fiction. Lalitaditya had very much patronized Buddhism during his reign. Ou-kong mentions existence of many Stupas and Viharas which he saw during his visit. These were by the side of numerous Vishnu shrines erected by him. The greatest Buddhist gift of the King was a great Vihara at Parihaspura with a colossal Buddha image which still existed in Kalhans time. There was another Vihara at Huskapura where Ou-kong stayed on his arrival in Kashmir. Llitaditya's end is also surrounded in mystery. There are many theories about his death but all point towards the fact that it occurred during his expedition in the northern region. According to one version he perished through excessive snow in a country called Aryanka which has not been exactly located. Another version states that he committed suicide after being separated from his army on a difficult mountain route. Some versions state that he retired along with his army to the world of immortals in the north. However, from all these accounts it may be concluded that Lalitaditya, the Alexander of Kashmir died on one of his conquering expeditions in the northern region. The maxims of policy which the King had set forth influenced Kashmir administration for a long time. Thus this very illustrious King of Kashmir had a tragic end similar to Alexander the great who also died on way back to Greece after his long trail of conquests

CHAPTER NINE

JAYAPIDA(GRANDSON OF LALITADITYA)

Jayapida (Grandson of Lalitaditya)

Who killed a lion with any arms to save the people of city of Panudarvardhana which was in the possession of Jayanta.The king of the city came to know that this lion had been killed by Jyapida. The king had no son but only a daughter, named Kalyani Devi. He married her to

Jyapida. Jayapida was none other than the youngest grandson Lalitaditya. He defeated his elder brother Samranpida and ascended the throne. Jyapida reign can be divided into two parts. In the first part he ruled with kindness and justice and established peace and order in the country. The people achieved prosperity in every field. But in the last years of his life he became a tyrant and indulged in loot and plunder. As soon as Jayapida sat on the throne, he made his aim to follow on the footsteps of Lalitaditya. He resolved that he could like him make conquests and make Kashmir affluent and prosperous. Kalhana says that Jayapida was very noble and loved justice. The first notable thing that he did was that he established peace and order and also made good arrangement for the governance of the country. He collected a large army and set out on expeditions. Many soldiers who were not so loyal and were restless to go to their homes left him day by day but this brave king determined that he would show his personal bravery. Kalhana writes that Jyapida in his early expedition conquered many places up to Allahabad. At Prayag or Allahabad he gave in charity 10,000 horses and wealth as alms to the priests. On the bank of the Ganges he got built a memorial which still existed in the life time of Kalhana. After this he put his army under the command of his minister Devasarman and Himself entered incognito all alone in the city of Panudarvardhana which was in the possession of Jayanta. In this city there was much peace and prosperity and people were affluent. He was highly pleased to see the condition of the people. In this city a ferocious lion would come every night and eat men and animals. Jyapida killed this lion without the aid of arms. The king of the city came to know that this lion had been killed by Jyapida. The king had no son but only a daughter, named Kalyani Devi. He married her to Jyapida. After that both the king and Jyapida subjugated all the neighboring kings. On his return to Kashmir, Jyapida defeated the king of Kanauj, Vajrayudha. When Jyapida arrived in Kashmir, he found that during his three years' absence his first wife's brother had usurped his throne. He fought and defeated him at Subseletra. Kalhana mentions that all the people from far and near came and joined his army. During the fight a Candala soldier of Jyapida, named Shri Deva, killed Jojja, who was drinking water from a gold pot astride a horse. As soon as Shri Deva saw the latter he threw a stone at him with such a force that he died on the spot. It is well worthy to mention about the construction activities of Jyapida. He founded a city named Jaipura near the Wular Lake. This city is today known as Andarkot. He also constructed a fort there. It was surrounded by a marshy land and it was difficult to conquer it. In the later history of the valley many important battles were fought there. Two more towns were founded by Jyapida. One was named as Dvarvati which was near Jaipura. The second one was called Malhanpura which at present is called Malur. It is situated at a distance of six miles from Srinagar on the left bank of the river Jhelum. The two queens of the king, named Kalyani Devi and Kamla Devi, also founded two towns. One was known as Kalyanpur and the other Kamalapur. One of his ministers called Jayadita constructed a matha in Jaipura. The king was a patron of art and literature. He invited scholars and learned men from other countries. He reestablished the education of the classical language. He himself studied grammar under the guidance of a learned man, named Kshera. His special Pandit was one great scholar Bhatta Udbhatta, whom he paid one lakh dinars daily. He appointed as his special minister one poet Damodhar Gupta who has written Kuttanimatta. There were poets and authors like Manoratha, Sankha Danta, Katika and Samdhima who occupied places of honor in his court. Among the ministers of Jyapida was Vaman, one of the two authors of the famous book Kashikavrtti. This book is a commentary on Panini's grammar. He also raised the status of Thakkiya, a writer from low position and helped and patronized him for his knowledge and learning. We know some of these people from their books and references. In Rajatarangini it is mentioned that under the leadership of Jyapida his army attacked Bhim Sen, the king of the northern region. But he imprisoned Jyapida who, however, escaped from the prison by a subtle plan, pretending that he was suffering from a terrible infectious disease. It is said that he then attacked Nepal's ruler Aramudi but he was carried away by the sudden spate in a river and his enemies arrested him. He was imprisoned in a strong fort but he fled away due to the loyalty and self sacrifice of Devasarman, a minister. Devasarman killed himself so that Jyapida could take the help of his dead body after jumping from the fort and be able to cross the river, where the army was waiting for him. But neither Bhimsen nor Aramudi was traced. However, considering the confusing and chaotic condition prevailing in northern India, it does not seem impossible that he fought in those areas. The result of all these expeditions was that his slender resources were nearly exhausted and the money in the treasury also dwindled, particularly when he could not get anything by loot or plunder or by levying tax which he expected. The story that a Naga deity of the Wular Lake directed him to a copper mine nearby shows how much in need of money he was so that he could carry on the administration and pay the salaries of his soldiers. There is nothing surprising in the fact that in the last years of his life he became very cruel and squeezed out every penny from his people. In this respect he was helped by his Revenue minister, Shiv Das. Continuously for three years he took control of the produce from the land which included the portion of the peasants as welt. Murder and loot became quite rampant. The people felt miserable. The one who ought to have been their defender, turned out to be their plunderer and murderer

CHAPTER TEN

AVANTIVARMAN(DEVELOPMENT MAN OF KASHMIR)

Avantivarman (Kashmir's Development Man)

In the history of Kashmir, the Utpala dynasty holds a special place. The founder of the Utpala dynasty was Avantivarman who ruled from AD 855 to 883. He was more interested in internal administration than military conquests. New towns and irrigation works were constructed One of these towns was Suyyapura called after his minister and engineer Suyya who gave a further impetus to the agriculture of Kashmir by draining marshes and protecting the fields against the deluge of avalanches. It is said of Suyya that he made the streams of Indus and Jhelum flow according to his will, like a snake charmer his snakes. Avantivarman founded a new city Avantipur. A patron of learning, Avantivarman, in his court, has two poets, Ratnakara and Anandavardhan. In his time, according to the Kashmiri poet Kalhana, author of Rajatarangini rice was sold for 36 dinars per khari, as against 2000 dinar as earlier, showing the revival of the country's prosperity

A King's Passion for Art & Learning

Though of an inglorious lineage, Avantivarman made himself illustrious by virtue of his peaceful pursuits, conscientious care of his subjects and liberal patronage of arts and learning He did not launch on an ambitious career of conquests. Aided by his wise and faithful minister Sura, the great king devoted his energies to the consolidation of his kingdom by subduing the unruly opponents and turbulent chiefs and brought back the much needed peace and prosperity to the country, hitherto town by court intrigues, factions and oppression of the subjects during the reign of the later feeble puppet kings of the Karakota dynasty.

He made earnest efforts to ameliorate the economic condition of the people and picked up a gifted person, Suyya, who by his engineering operations regulated the course of the Vitasta, thereby arresting the devastating periodical floods and consequent famine, and promoted irrigation and agricultural operations over an extensive area with the result that output of crops increased tremendously. His court was adorned by men of learning and poets like "Muktakana", "Shivasvamin", "Anandavardhan" and "Ratnakara". His just and peaceful rule of twenty-eight years was made further memorable by a large number of religious foundations and endowments, not only by himself but by his relatives and officials.

Building Of the Two Temples

At Avantipura itself Avantivarman erected two magnificent temples, one dedicated to Lord Vishnu called "Avantivarman" and the other to Lord Shiva called "Avantisvara" the former built before his accession to the throne and the latter after obtaining sovereignty. The king was a devout worshipper of Lord Vishnu from his childhood and remained Vaishnava in the core of his heart till his death. However, out of great regard for his minister Sura who was a devotee of Shiva, he made the other temple dedicated to Lord Shiva.

After the seventh century, Hinduism was receiving more attention of scholars in Kashmir and in the centuries that followed, Kashmir produced many poets, philosophers, and artists who contributed to Hindu religion and Sanskrit literature. Among notable scholars of this period was Vasugupta (875–925 CE) who wrote the Shiva Sutras which laid the foundation for a monastic Shiva system called Kashmiri Shaivism. Soon Kashmir Shaivism came to dominate lives of ordinary people in Kashmir largely at the expense of Buddhism

CHAPTER ELEVEN

QUEEN SUGANDHA(904-906 AD)

Sugandha (904-906 AD)

Sugndha Rani was one of the four queens to have ruled Kashmir. She ascended the throne after her husband Sankara Varman died in battle and her son Gopala Varman was murdered. Sugandha was the daughter of Svamiraja, the king of a kingdom near Kashmir and he had at-least three other queens including one Surendravati. Sugandha was married to Sankaravarman, who reigned as King of Kashmir from 885 AD to 902 AD. During this time, Sugandha acted as his consort. Sankaravarman died in 902 of a stray-arrow at Urusha (present-day Hazara, Pakistan), whilst returning from a not-so-successful conquest, where Sugandha had also accompanied him. Following his death, he was succeeded by his son, Gopalavarman. While some of Sankaravarman queens and servants died by Sati, the Dowager Queen Sugandha refused it so as to act as Queen Mother and regent for Gopalavarman. After Sankaravarmans last rites had finished, Gopalavarman was crowned the King of Kashmir. Although Sugandha was good at managing the affairs of the kingdom, she took pleasure in bodily indulgences. Various historians accuse her of being intimate to her treasury minister Prabhakaradeva, who they describe as her paramour. Prabhakaradeva used to exercise the real powers of the King. He engaged in prolonged theft of state-treasures and was finally probed by Gopalavarman. In due course, Prabhakaradeva employed a relative Ramadeva to assassinate the king by slow poisoning. Gopalavarman died of a fever and Ramadeva committed suicide, after his conspiracy became public knowledge. After Gopalavarman's death, his brother Sankata became King but he died mysteriously after ten days. After Sankaravarmans lineage died out, Kashmir fell into a political turmoil. Courtiers started plotting a coup and public figures called a Maha-Panchayat to choose the kingdom's ruler. As Sugandha was quite popular among the people, she was proclaimed the sovereign of Kashmir.

In 904 AD Sugandha assumed royal power and ruled Kashmir in her own right. Some historians believe that she did it apparently with an intention of securing it for her grandson the yet-unborn child of Jayalakshmi.She ruled Kashmir for two years (904 – 906 AD).

She hoped that she would be succeeded by her unborn grandson, the son of Gopalavarman but Jayalakshmi.She pregnancy resulted in a stillbirth. Sugandha, now in despair, wished that she be succeeded by one of her blood-relatives, Nirjitavarman, a grandson of Suravarman and a half-brother of Avantivarman, nicknamed Pangu (lame). She nominated Pangu to the throne and in doing this; she had to seek the advice and permission of her ministers. Sugandha's choice was met with considerable resistance from the ministers as well as the Tantrins, on grounds of Nirjitavarmans lameness. Sugandha was dethroned by the Tantrins and they installed Nirjitavarmans ten-year-old son Partha as monarch instead. Following her dethronement in

906 AD, Sugandha continued to claim the throne of Kashmir and retreated to live in Huskapura (present-day Ushkur, Baramulla).

In 914, after eight years of exile in Huskapura, Sugandha was persuaded by the Ekangas, Royal bodyguards and other factions loyal to her, to wage a war against Partha and the Tantrins. The fierce battle occurred in the suburbs of Srinagar in April 914 AD. She was defeated and captured by the Tantrins. Sugandha was imprisoned and later killed in a Buddhist monastery called Nispalaka Vihara.

Sugandha's reign constitutes the first concrete and historically verifiable reign of a female sovereign in Kashmir's history and ruled at the behest of her subjects. During her reign, Sugandha built the towns of Sugandhapura and Gopalapura, the Vishnu temple Gopalakesava, and the monastery of Gopalamatha. She also built the Sugandesha Temple, located at Pattan, which has a square sanctum with a portico in front and a peristyle around. Sankaravarman, along with Sugandha, dedicated two temples to Mahadeva, namely Sankara Gauresa and Sugandhesvara at the new capital of Sankarapura. These two stately temples are still standing today at modern-day Pattan. Sugandha's coinage is an important corroborative evidence of her in her coins Goddess Lakshmi is seen seated in Lalitasana in most of the coins and Sharda script is distinctly visible.

CHAPTER TWELVE

SHIVA PHILOSOPHY OF KASHMIR

Shiva philosophy of Kashmir (Revival of Hinduism in Kashmir in 8th to 12th century AD)

It was the 9th century revival of Hinduism started relatively new farm of Shiva philosophy came to existence which was entirely different this revolution of Shaivism of Kashmir has developed between the eight and the twelfth centuries of the Christian era. This comparatively younger philosophy has tried to explain all such ambiguities which the ancient philosophers have failed to resolve. Vasugupta was a ninth century author who is best known for writing the Shiva Sutras, an important text in the Advaita tradition of Kashmir Shaivism, which is also known as Trika or Trika Yoga. Some even regard Vasugupta as the founder of this tradition. The details of Vasugupta's life are not well known. According to references to his work in other texts and the better known details of his students, it is believed Vasugupta lived in the first half of the ninth century. In the Shiva tradition, Vasugupta is believed to have amassed his knowledge and recognition through direct realization. Vasugupta's students included Kallata and Somananda, both of whom themselves composed philosophical texts sometime between 825 and 900 CE. Kallata was his principal disciple and spread the Shiva Sutras. Vasugupta's Shiva Sutras explore the nature and causes of bondage, and how one can be liberated from this bondage. He also wrote the Spanda Karakas, a commentary on his Shiva Sutras. After him tradition and knowledge was enriched by Utpaladeva (c. 925-975 AD) and Abhinavagupt (975-1025). AbhinavGupt's disciple Kshemaraja (1000-1050 AD) and other successors interpreted that philosophy as defining retrospectively the significance of earlier monistic Shiva theology and philosophy.

Silent features of Kashmir Shaivism

Lord Shiva is the nature and existence of all beings. The external objective world is expansion of his Energy and it is filled with the glamour of the glory of God Consciousness. In other words, bigness or existence itself is awareness. The appearing of an objective world occurs within this subjectivity due to its own creative activity, personified as Shakti.The diverse manifestations of life are celebrated in Kashmir Shaivism. In some traditions Kashmir Shivite adepts refer to our world and all worlds as ornaments of God or as the glamour or magical appearing of God. Our sense of separation is the source of our suffering. Once we are consciously immersed in living presence, seeing the wisdom in all that is we can enjoy the diversity of life. In Kashmir Shaivism, the myriad productions of God have a fundamentally aesthetic, self-expressive nature. As we wake up more, we also become more freely expressive. Ultimately we discover that that everything is made of and expressive of a playful and vast intelligence, a vast compassion, utterly devotional and operating with unimaginable responsively and clarity. Manifest life is a no-holds-barred conversation of Self with Self. Nature's conversation is multi-dimensional and infinite. Practices such as mantra, kriya yoga, meditation, and working with an accomplished teacher erode our sense of separateness and stabilizes our senses. Over time, we become more aware of and sensitive to our continuity with the pervasive Self and its call and response playfulness. As our body, energy, and mind wake up, we regain our capacity for embodying natural wisdom virtues such as creativity, compassion, wonder, and devotion. We become more skillful players in life's tender game. From the start of your journey until you realize that there was never a journey after all, it is the advent of direct understanding of self and the embodiment of wisdom virtues that is our beacon and our goal.

Vasugupta

Little is known about Vasugupta's life, other than he lived in Kashmir and in the first half of the 9th century. He probably was born in late 8th century. This dating is based on mentions of his work in other Indian texts, and the biography of his students particularly Kallata and Somananda, both of whom are dated to have actively composed philosophical texts sometime between 825 and 900 AD m .He probably was a contemporary and aware of the ideas of Advaita Vedanta, and of Buddhist scholars of the 8th and 9th century.

The author is believed in Shiva tradition to have amassed knowledge and recognition through direct realization. He was a native of Kashmir and a Shiva. It is unclear how and what inspired him to write the Shiva Sutras, and early texts mention no legends. Later tradition and hagiographic texts present inconsistent stories. One states that Vasugupta found the sutras inscribed on a rock called Sankaropala. Other state that Shiva appeared in his dream and recited it to him, who then wrote it down. There are additional stories, but the texts of the immediate students of Vasugupta mention none of these legends except the one where Vasugupta discovers the Sutras in his dream.

Vasugupta also wrote the Spanda Karikas as a commentary on the Shiva Sutras. He paved the way for later scholars for a cultural and religious renaissance in Kashmir which continued for centuries till the advent of Islam. His principal disciple, Bhatta Kallata spread the Shiva Sutras, and wrote Spanda-karika in the 2nd half of the 9th century.

Abhinavagupt (950 – 1016 AD)

Abhinavagupt was born in 950 AD in Kashmir and died in 1020 AD. He was a philosopher, musician, poet and dramatist. He exercised strong influences on Kashmiri Shivite culture. Abhinavagupt was not his real name, rather a title he earned from his master, carrying a meaning of competence and authoritativeness

Family

Abhinavagupt was born in a Kashmiri Brahmin family. His mother died when Abhinavagupt was just two years old as a consequence of losing his mother, of whom he was reportedly much attached, he grew more distant from worldly life and focused all the more on spiritual Endeavour. The father, Narasiṃha Gupta, after his wife's death favored an ascetic lifestyle, while raising his three children. He had a cultivated mind and a heart "outstandingly adorned with devotion Shiva. Abhinavagupt had a brother and a sister. The brother, Manoratha, was a well-versed devotee of Shiva. His sister devoted herself to worship after the death of her husband in late life. His cousin Karṇa demonstrated even from his youth that he grasped the essence of Shaivism and was detached of the world.

Ancestors

By Abhinavagupt own account, his most remote known ancestor was called Atrigupta, born in Madhyadesh region according to him 200 years ago from his birth had settled in Kashmir during the reign of Lalitaditya Ruler of Kashmir whose empire extended up to Kanauj territory of present Uttar Pradesh State. At that time, his forefather Abhigupt was a renowned scholar and King Lalitaditya who was found of Scholars requested him to settle in Kashmir. He accepted his request and King Lalitaditya granted him great estate and built a house for him.

Life Style

Abhinavagupt was the progeny of parents who had established themselves in divine essence and from childhood. His mother died when he was just 2 years old and his father afterwards favored spiritual path. His father was his first Guru who instructed him in Sanskrit grammar, logic and literature. His brother and sister were also ardent devotees of Lord Shiva. He had more than 15 gurus and tried to grab knowledge from anybody whose ideas appealed to him. That house during AbhinavGupt's period had become an Ashram where great scholars of that time from Kashmir used to assemble (both males and females) and frequent discussions on religious matters were taking place. He remained unmarried all his life and used his energy. He travelled mostly inside Kashmir. He did not take on regular duties of his family and lived his life as a writer and a teacher. He has authored between 35-49 literary works and TantraLok is the most important work on Shaivism which is considered as encyclopedia. Abhinavagupt took with him 1200 disciples and marched off to a cave which is known as Bhairava Cave situated in village Magam and it exists there even at present. He made an entry in the cave by reciting his poem Bhairava, Stava, a devotional work. They were never to be seen again

CHAPTER THIRTEEN

QUEEN DIDDA(IRON LADY OF KASHMIR)

Queen Didda of Kashmir (Iron lady of Kashmir)

She was only ruler Mohammad Ghazni feared and never mastered courage to attack Kashmir during his time he attacked Kashmir twice after his death but was defeated both times. It was not easy for these Queens to rule with an Iron grip .But they somehow managed and found their own place in the History of Kashmir. One Such Lady who rose against all the odds and decimated her enemies and till date she retains her position of number one the Queen whose rule spanned for almost half a decade.

Queen Didda was married to King Ksemagupta (950-958 A.D) of Kashmir. She was the daughter of King Simharaja.The lord of Lohara and Grand Daughter of King Bhima-Sahi of Kabul. She had transfixed the King Ksemagupta, and had wholly engrossed his mind. The King had engraved the image of Didda on the coins and was thus also known as DIDDAKSEMA.It was a derogatory appellation used for Ksemagupta. The King was also married to Candralekha The daughter of his Minister (Dvarapati) Phalguna. Didda had developed an animosity towards the minister. Didda gave birth to a son Abhimanyu and her grandfather the powerful Bhima-Shahi, visited Kashmir to see his great grandson. Bhima Shahi built a temple Bhimakeshava near Martanda. In 958, Ksemagupta contracted a violent fever during one of his beloved jackal hunts. He was taken to the Kshemamatha in Varahamula (Baramulla) and died there.

Didda immediately secreted away her son in case he was killed. She was now on her own surrounded by threats to her own life and to her son's. The first challenge came when the courtiers gathered for the funeral, and there was great pressure on Didda to commit sati along with the other queens who included Phalguna daughter. She refused, saying she had to live to protect her son. Abhimanyu was then crowned and she became the regent.

The first direct challenge she faced was from Kshemagupta's sister's sons, Mahiman and Patala. They gathered many allies especially Brahmins from Lalitadityapur and surrounded her when she was visiting the Padmasvamin temple. She managed to get her son away to a math and then asked to negotiate. During the negotiations she managed to bribe some of the supporters and placate others. Her faithful minister Naravahana then won a victory over the rest. She ruthlessly killed off many of the rebels including her husband's nephews but forgave some she thought would be of use to her.

One of them was the warrior Yashodhara whom she sent to subdue Thakkana, the ruler of a neighboring kingdom of Shahi descent. Yashodhara won but let Thakkana retain his kingdom. Yashodhara came back expecting a hero's welcome, but instead there was a botched-up attempt by Didda to arrest him.

Yashodhara immediately revolted, and many nobles joined him. This was perhaps the toughest revolt Didda faced, but she managed to suppress it with the help of her ministers Naravahana and Rakka. Again, the rebels and their relatives were brutally killed.

In 972, Abhimanyu, her only child, died. His minor son Nandigupta was crowned, and Didda continued as regent.

For a year, grief-stricken, she immersed herself in an orgy of building, especially to commemorate her son. She built the Abhimanyusvamin temple and Abhimanyupura town, which is now called Bimyan. She built the Diddasvamin temple, the Diddapura town, and the Diddamath, now called the Diddmar area of Srinagar. By one estimate, she laid 64 foundations.

But Nandigupta fell sick and died in a year, followed in quick succession by the next grandson Tribhuvangupta, who had been crowned by her in 973. Many accused Didda of witchcraft in bringing about their deaths, but this is likely to be bad press, as she clearly had nothing to gain by doing so. She crowned the third grandson Bhimagupta in 975. After his death Didda ruled for the next 22 years in absolute power until she died in 1003 at the age of 79, quashing rebellions periodically by using her standard combination of bribes, appeasement and ferocious reprisal.

Phalguna, her Chief Minister and the mainstay of her administration, died during Bhimagupta reign. There was a new twist in her life at this point with the entry of a young man Tunga. Tunga was a buffalo herdsman from Poonch, who had come to Kashmir with his brothers and was employed as a letter carrier in her government. Impressed by his capabilities she started promoting him until he finally became Prime Minister and commander of the armies. He actually continued to capably hold these posts for nearly 40 years, even after her death. He was widely considered to be her lover, though she was more than 50 years old by the time she met him.

CHAPTER FOURTEEN

SANGRAMA RAJA

Sangrama Raja (1003-1028 AD).

Who defeated Mohammad Ghazni twice and forced him to run like rat. He was Queen Didda's nephew aware of all the policies made by Didda in her last years and he supported Hindus against Muhammad Ghazni with an army under the Minister of Tunga. After the death of Queen Didda's Muhammad Ghazni mastered the courage to attack Kashmir but Mahmood Ghazni attacked many Indian borders, he attacked many cities of India after conquering the Kangra fort; his vulture came near the free state of Kashmir!

He invaded Kashmir in 1015 AD with the intention of conquering this state too. The information of Mahmud's attack was increased in the border areas, due to the vigilance and the activities of the detectives immediately reached the king! Kashmir's army headed under the leadership of an accomplished commander Tung! The kingdom of Trilochanpal was on the Kabul state with the state of Kashmir .King Trilochanpal himself also came in the field of Tausi with the army. Mahmood Ghazni army was surrounded by soldiers from both sides of the mountains! In spite of all the deceit, cunning conspiracy and ambush rebounds, Mahmud had been adopting it in earlier battles from now; all of them were left behind .Surrounded the escape to find a way to find the way. The equation of Kashmir and Kabul was that the enemy was shown stars in the day. Tausi war zone of Kashmir became witness to the defense of freedom struggle and self-respect and our soldiers slaughtered the dead bodies in the war zone by killing thousands of enemies. Mahmood Ghazni was captured on the fort of Lohkot by Army of Sangram Raj broke the fort and entered the fort! Mahmud was very scared to see Indian soldiers entering the fort. So he hid in a safe place! Mahmud Ghazni could somehow succeed in escaping his life! In the Cambridge History of India, this war has been described as a very interesting one. Mahmood first and biggest defeat in India his army forget the path on unfamiliar mountain routes and the way back to it was stopped by flood water but after the massive loss of life his army managed to reach Ghazni.

With this defeat in Kashmir, He forgot his resolve to attack India every year and after six years, in 1021, he again attacked Kashmir! Every year the invading attacker returned the courage to attack Kashmir in six years. It is clear that Tausi's war zone was long remembered even in 1021 Ghazni. Stayed on the Lohaghat

As soon as Trilochanpal realized Mahmud's invasion, he started a campaign to repeal it immediately Maharaja Sangram Raj sent his army to help Trilochanpal Pal! Mahmood was reminded of his previous defeat! He kept on keeping his feet in the Kashmir Valley of India with the help of the previous wounds that the unexpected hit started again! He started to experience the previous experience within! This time the situation had become the same, from both sides were surrounded by the freedom fighter army of Trilochanpal Pal and Maharaja Sangramraj.To save his life Mahmud Ghazni had to be turned away from Kashmir to Ghazni. He was succeeded by his son Ananta Deva (1028-1063 AD) & his grandson Kalasha (1063-1089 AD).

CHAPTER FIFTEEN

KING HARSHA

King Harsha

From 1089 to 1101 A. D King Harsha ruled Kashmir. Versed in many languages, a good poet, lover of music and art, he started his rule in a remarkable way, and became famous in northern India. His court was a centre of luxury and splendor. He introduced new fashions in dress and ornaments. His ministers were gorgeously dressed, wore earrings and head dresses, previously reserved for the members of ruling families only. But strangely enough, Harsha's career became a record of follies and misdeeds. The people also suffered from famine, and plague as well, and a considerable section of people became victims of these calamities. Confusion followed these misfortunes, leading to a general rising of the people under two royal princes Uccalia and Succalla. Harsha along with his son Bhoja were murdered. Harsha and is probably one king who Kalhana has painted despicably. Kalhana's Rajatarangini gives an interesting account of Harsha. Kalhana's father Champaka was a minister of Harsha. Kalhana wrote during the time of Jayasimha (AD 1127-59).He looted both Hindu and Buddhist temples, and is credited with creating an office of devotpaatana-nayaka who used to loot the gold from the temples. In Kalhana's time, Buddhism was flourishing in Kashmir, and was not considered a distinct religion from Hinduism. He refers to Buddhists' idols just like Brahmnaical ones. During his time there were too many famines due to flooding. The merchant who exported rice to Kashmir used to charge 20 to 50 times more. Dissolute king Harsha when in financial straits was advised by his evil counselor Lotsdhara to restore his fortunes by looting the temples and melting down the images of the gods. There is nothing to prove that he destroyed temples to promote his faith or ideology (Hinduism). He looted both Hindu and Buddhist temples and never ever massacred Buddhist community which left wing writers want to portray him. Harsha although he did destroy temples and Viharas but the reason, was not to promote Hinduism or to subjugate Buddhism. What however can be argued is that he may be doing at the behest of whom Kalhana calls Turks (outsiders/foreigners who were Muslims in this case) what later Muslim kings did i.e., try and destroy the very root of Hinduism . Kalhana calls him a Turushka (Turk). He had put every hundreds of his soldiers under the command of a Turk warrior (they could have been Muslims). Harsha apparently reneged from Hinduism, but he could not have embraced Islam. He ate it is claimed porcine food. He did however choose Turkish style of dress for his soldiers. What is more, if at all one wants to compare Harsha's behavior with that of the Muslim rulers, one should face the connection that the contemporary historian Kalhan explicitly makes. Kalhan is simply saying that the very idea that a temple need not be respected was borrowed by Harsha from the Muslim Turks. These already had a well-established reputation for temple desecration, and that is a fact to which the historians prefer not to d raw the reader's attention.

CHAPTER SIXTEEN

LOHARA DYNASTY

Lohara Dynasty

According Kalhan Lohara dynasty would always remembered by the victory of Sangramraj who defeated over the Mohammad Ghazanavi but the future generation of this dynasty turned out to be very cruel and character less . Worst of them was King Harsha. Harsha and is probably one king who Kalhana has painted despicably

Queen Didda of Lohara (958-972 AD) became queen in 958 AD after the death of her husband Ksemagupta to protect the rights of her son Abhimanyu. She was a good administrator with far sighted policies that made her the actual founder of the dynasty. Her alliance with the Empire of Sahis in Afghanistan and Punjab also gave her the support of local King Bhima Deva which made her throne stronger .After few years realizing full well that she was ageing and nobody from her own dynasty was living to succeed her. She soon started looking for her successor and her choice narrowed down to Samgramaraja the son of his brother Udyaraja. Samgramaraja was appointed as Yuvraj by her and in 1003 AD after her death, Samgramaraja became the king establishing Lohara dynasty in Kashmir. He was Queen Didda's nephew aware of all the policies made by Didda in her last years. He thrashed Muhammad Ghazni with an army under the Minister of Tunga. Kashmir was met with an attack two times and Sangrama had to defend it against Ghazni. Who defeated Mohammad Ghazni twice and forced him to run like rat. He was Queen Didda's nephew aware of all the policies made by Didda in her last years and he supported Hindus against Muhammad Ghazni with an army under the Minister of Tunga. After the death of Queen Didda's Muhammad Ghazni mastered the courage to attack Kashmir but Mahmood Ghazni attacked many Indian borders, he attacked many cities of India after conquering the Kangra fort; his vulture came near the free state of Kashmir. He invaded Kashmir in

1015 AD with the intention of conquering this state too. The information of Mahmud's attack was increased in the border areas, due to the vigilance and the activities of the detectives immediately reached the king. Kashmir's army headed under the leadership of an accomplished commander Tung .The kingdom of Trilochanpal was on the Kabul state with the state of Kashmir .King Trilochanpal himself also came in the field of Tausi with the army. Mahmood Ghazni army was surrounded by soldiers from both sides of the mountains! In spite of all the deceit, cunning conspiracy and ambush rebounds, Mahmud had been adopting it in earlier battles from now; all of them were left behind .Surrounded the escape to find a way to find the way. The equation of Kashmir and Kabul was that the enemy was shown stars in the day. Tausi war zone of Kashmir became witness to the defense of freedom struggle and self-respect and our soldiers slaughtered the dead bodies in the war zone by killing thousands of enemies. Mahmood Ghazni was captured on the fort of Lohkot by Army of Sangram Raj broke the fort and entered the fort. Mahmud was very scared to see Indian soldiers entering the fort. So he hid in a safe place Ghazni could somehow succeed in escaping his life. Mahmood first and biggest defeat in India his army forget the path on unfamiliar mountain routes and the way back to it was stopped by flood water but after the massive loss of life his army managed to reach Ghazni. With this defeat in Kashmir, He forgot his resolve to attack India every year and after six years, in 1021, he again attacked Kashmir! Every year the invading attacker returned the courage to attack Kashmir in six years. It is clear that Tausi's war zone was long remembered even in 1021 Ghazni. Stayed on the Lohaghat As soon as Trilochanpal realized Mahmud's invasion, he started a campaign to repeal it immediately Maharaja Sangram Raj sent his army to help Trilochanpal Pal! Mahmood was reminded of his previous defeat! He kept on keeping his feet in the Kashmir Valley of India with the help of the previous wounds that the unexpected hit started again! He started to experience the previous experience within. This time the situation had become the same, from both sides were surrounded by the freedom fighter army of Trilochanpal Pal and Maharaja Sangramraj.To save his life Mahmud Ghazni had to be turned away from Kashmir to Ghazni. He was succeeded by his son Ananta Deva (1028-1063 AD) & his grandson Kalasha (1063-1089 AD).Kalasha's sons Utkarsha and Harsha were unable to get along due to their personal egoistic, self-centered and hostile nature. But being the elder son Utkarsha was been made the king, however, Harsha was more capable and visionary than him. Harsha and is probably one king who Kalhana has painted despicably. Kalhana's Rajatarangini gives an interesting account of Harsha. Kalhana's father Champaka was a minister of Harsha. Kalhana wrote during the time of Jayasimha (AD 1127-59).He looted both Hindu and Buddhist temples, and is credited with creating an office of devotpaatana-nayaka who used to loot the gold from the temples. In Kalhana's time, Buddhism was flourishing in Kashmir, and was not considered a distinct religion from Hinduism. He refers to Buddhists' idols just like Brahmnaical ones. During his time there were too many famines due to flooding. The merchant who exported rice to Kashmir used to charge 20 to 50 times more. Dissolute king Harsha when in financial straits was advised by his evil counselor Lotsdhara to restore his fortunes by looting the temples and melting down the images of the gods. There is nothing to prove that he destroyed temples to promote his faith or ideology (Hinduism). He looted both Hindu and Buddhist temples and never ever massacred Buddhist community which left wing writers want to portray him. Harsha although he did destroy temples and Viharas but the reason, was not to promote Hinduism or to subjugate Buddhism. What however can be argued is that he may be doing at the behest of whom Kalhana calls Turks (outsiders/foreigners who were Muslims in this case) what later Muslim kings did i.e., try and destroy the very root of Hinduism . Kalhana calls him a Turushka (Turk). He had put every hundreds of his soldiers under the command of a Turk warrior (they could have been Muslims). Harsha apparently reneged from Hinduism, but he could not have embraced Islam. He ate it is claimed porcine food. He did however choose Turkish style of dress for his soldiers. What is more, if at all one wants to compare Harsha's behavior with that of the Muslim rulers, one should face the connection that the contemporary historian Kalhan explicitly makes. Kalhan is simply saying that the very idea that a temple need not be respected was borrowed by Harsha from the Muslim Turks. These already had a well-established reputation for temple desecration, and that is a fact to which the historians prefer not to draw the readers 'attention. After Harsha's death the downfall started as no one could rule with the full power and authority. Later Uchchala (1001-11 AD), a descendant of Didda's brother came to power. His Brother Sussala (1128 AD) and then his son (1155 AD) ruled Kashmir. But they were always led down by their relatives. In the last, Jayasimha took over the charge; due to fight among selves the dynasty came to end in 1171 AD. During this time, a large number of Muslims joined the army and took over many administrative positions. However, it took them more than 200 years to become the rulers.

CHAPTER SEVENTEEN

KALHANA

Kalhana and Rajtarangini

Kalhana was one of the earliest Kashmiri writers who made a significant contribution not only to Kashmiri literature but all of ancient Indian literature as well. Kalhana is best known for his work Rajatarangini. Kalhana wrote Rajtarangni only because of patriotism and love for his country. He was also inspired by regional patriotism. By painting a glorious picture of the past he wished that the countrymen should shed their inferiority complex, feel proud and try to follow their past traditions. In the 12th century this man decided to write for the purpose of history, and as a historian. Kalhana is regarded as the first historian of India. In 1148 Kalhana started writing the history of the rulers of Kashmir, starting from legends to the kings and queens of the 12th century. It took him two years to complete the book and in 1150 AD he had completed the Rajtarangini the River of Kings. Very little is known about Kalhana. He was the son of Champaka, a minister in the employ of King Harsha of Kashmir (1089-1101 AD). Champaka is referred in Rajatarangini as Dvarapati or the Lord of the Gates commander of the frontier troops. Kalhana was born in Parihaspura now known as Paraspore in the Baramulla district of Jammu & Kashmir. The introductory note attached to the end of each book of Rajatarangini, gives the name of the author as Kalhana the son of the great Kashmiri Minister the illustrious Lord Champaka. Historical deductions reveal that he was a Brahmin by caste. The name Kalhana was derived through the Prakrit Kalhan from the Sanskrit language word Kalyana meaning blessed. Kalhana wrote his work during the years 1148-1149. The style and the spirit of the work show that the author must have attained a mature age. The elaborate description of the unsteady conditions of Sussal's reign (1112-20) makes it clear that he must have been of age at that time. Hence, his probable date of birth might have been the beginning of the twelfth century. Kalhana's birth century was an important historical period in Kashmir. It was a period of extreme dynastic upheaval resulting in many political changes. King Harsha (1089-1101) seemed at first to give Kashmir a period of good government but he fell victim to his own lavishness and extravagances at the end worst of the kings .After his murder Kashmir for seven years more, witnessed civil wars which brought death and destruction in its wake. Kalhana was gifted with a scientific approach and a critical temperament. His portrayal of the various classes of Kashmiri people is very graphic and true to life. The reaction of the common folk to the disturbed political conditions of the time is full of realistic touches. He says that the people were zealously prepared to welcome any change. His description of the idle and indifferent city crowds and their feelings shows that he thoroughly understood the nature of his countrymen. Kalhana has honestly and impartially related the events. While recording the contemporary happenings Kalhana has presented the principal figures in their individual character and not as types.

It is interesting to note that Kalhana prepared himself for the role of a poet. The classical poetry in Sanskrit literature cultivated by Kalhana reveals that he had an intensive training in the Indian rhetoric, the Alankarshastra and the equal mastery of Sanskrit grammatical lore. His literary studies were deep and comprehensive. All the literature of his time, beginning from the Epics to Kalidasa's works Raghuvanisha and Meghaduta and Bilhan's Vikramankadevacharita and Hanshcharita, were read by him. It therefore appears that his literary training was of the strictly traditional type. Kalhana thoroughly studied the original sources including inscriptions of various kinds before he started writing, the Rajatarangini. He also studied coins and inspected buildings. Kalhana found all possible avenues to his hereditary career closed on account of unsettled political conditions of the country. So, the best way to employ his talents, he thought, was to write down the history of his country from ancient down to his time. He was also inspired by regional patriotism. By painting a glorious picture of the past he wished that the countrymen should shed their inferiority complex, feel proud and try to follow their past traditions. Therefore he shows through his works the kind of Kashmir, whose examples were to be followed.

Rajatarangini, which consists of 7,826 verses, is divided into eight books. Book I attempts to weave imaginary tales of Kashmir kings into epic legends. Gonanda was the first king and a contemporary and enemy of the Hindu deity Krishna. Traces of genuine history are also found, however, in references to the Mauryan emperors Asoka and Jalauka; the Buddhist Kushan kings Hushka (Huviska), Jushka (Vajheska), and Kanishka and Mihirakula a Huna king. Book II introduces a new line of kings not mentioned in any other authentic source, starting with Partapaditya I and ending with Aryaraja. Book III starts with an account of the reign of Meghavahana of the restored line of Gonanda and refers to the brief reign of Matrigupta, a supposed contemporary of Vikramaditya Harsha of Malwa. There too, legend is mixed with reality, and Toramana Huna is incorporated into the line of Meghavahana. The book closes with the establishment of the Karakota Naga dynasty by Durlabhaka Partapaditya II, and it is from Book IV on that Rajatarangini takes on the character of a dependable historical narrative. The Karakota line came to a close with the usurpation of the throne by Avantivarman, who started the Utpala dynasty in 855. In Books V and VI the history of the dynasty continues to 1003, when the kingdom of Kashmir passed on to a new dynasty, the Lohara. Book VII brings the narrative to the death of King Harsha (1101), and Book VIII deals with the stormy events between the death of Harsha and the stabilization of authority under Kalhana's contemporary Jayasimha (reigned 1128–49).

CHAPTER EIGHTEEN

THE DECLINE OF HINDU EMPIRE IN KASHMIR

The decline of the Hindu Empire in Kashmir

From 1089 to 1101 King Harsha ruled Kashmir. Harsha's career became a record of follies and misdeeds. The people also suffered from famine, and plague as well, and a considerable section of people became victims of these calamities. Confusion followed these misfortunes, leading to a general rising of the people under two royal princes Uccalia and Succalla. Harsha along with his son Bhoja were murdered, and the Kashmir throne passed into the hands of two princes respectively. Both the princes met the fate of Harsha and when our great historian Kalhan completed his Rajatarangini in 1149 - 50 King Jayasimha, the last great ruler of the Hindu times was ruling the state.

Jaisimha's (1128-55) early days were critical, because of the preceding civil wars and political unrest. Still the new ruler was able to maintain his firm rule for 27 years in comparative safety. The King repaired and restored many temples and shrines, and numerous other pious foundations were also made during his reign. The people after a long time heaved a sigh of relief. From 1155 - 1339, the Kashmir rulers remained busy only in intrigues, debauchery, and mutual quarrels. These incessant feuds, civil wars, risings and upheavals greatly weakened Hindu domination of Kashmir. The valley soon became a prey to Mongol and Turkish raiders, free booters and foreign adventurers. Quite naturally, the boundaries of the Kingdom got shrunk, and were reduced to the proper valley only. The Kabul valley Proutonsa (Poonch), Pajapuri (Rajouri) Kangra, Jammu, Kisthwar and Ladhak, one after the other threw-off their allegiance to the rulers of Kashmir.

In the beginning of 14th century a ferocious Mongol, Dulucha invaded the valley through its northern side Zojila Pass, with an army of 60,000 men. Like Taimur in the Punjab and Delhi, Dulucha carried sword and fire, destroyed towns and villages and slaughtered thousands. His savage attack practically ended the Hindu rule in Kashmir. A weak and worthless man Raja Sahadev was the ruler then. It was during his reign that three adventurers, Shah Mir from Swat (Tribal) territory on the borders of Afghanistan, Rinchin from Ladhak, and Lankar Chak from Dard territory near Gilgit came to Kashmir, and played a notable role in subsequentive political history of the valley. All the three men were granted Jagirs by the King. Rinchin for 3 years became the ruler of Kashmir, Shah Mir was the first ruler of Shah Miri-dynasty, and the descendants of Lankar Chak established Chak rule in the Kashmir.

The last Hindu ruler of Kashmir was Udyan Dev. It was his chief Queen Kota Rani, who practically governed the state. She was a very brave lady, shrewd and an able ruler. Though she tried her best to save her Kingdom, odds were too heavy for her. The valley was again invaded by a Mongol and Turk invader Achalla, but the Queen defeated him, and drove away all the foreign troops. In the confusion Rinchin, the Ladhaki prince, whom the Hindu religious leaders of the time refused to admit into their fold, organized an internal rising and seized the throne. Before his death, he embraced Islam. Finally another rising was led by Shah Mir, who defeated the queen at Jayapur (modern Sumbal). The defeat upset her and seeing the indifference of the Hindu grandees and general public, she stabbed herself to death, because Shah Mir wanted to marry her. Her death in 1339 paved the way for the establishment of Muslim rule in Kashmir.

CHAPTER NINETEEN

LAST QUEEN OF KASHMIR KOTRANI

LAST QUEEN OF KASHMIR KOTRANI

The invasions of Mahmud Ghazanavi shook the Indian soil to its depths, and though he failed to occupy Kashmir .Invasion made the Kashmir's very vigilant for their national defense. The threat of Muslim invasion was always present consequently they did not allow any foreigners to come in and kept the country closed to the entire outside world at least for the time being. But such a state of affairs could not continue for long. The trading classes both merchants and manufacturers who had carried on a brisk trade with the Punjab were hard hit by their isolation from external markets and a general unrest particularly in the cities was the outcome. The working classes in the cities were without employment and the peasantry sullen and resentful because of the prevailing turmoil. Such a state of affairs lasted up to the reign of Sahadev (1301-1320).What was required was a powerful hand that could restore peace and prosperity to the realm. During Suhadeva's reign many foreigners mainly Muslims, came into Kashmir. The chief amongst them was a Muslim missionary popularly known as Bulbul Shah who converted Rinchina a Tibetan prince settled as a refugee in Kashmir where he became king later. He was followed by Shah Mir who came in 1313 A. D. Sahadev received him well being the son of a renowned Muslim divine and bestowed a Jagirs upon him. Lankar Chak an adventurer also came during Suhadeva's reigned settled in Kashmir under Suhadeva's patronage. Dulucha a Tartar chief invaded Kashmir with an army of 70,000 strong. Sahadev fled towards Kisthwar leaving his kingdom to the tender mercies of the merciless invader. Dulucha ordered a massacre. Thousands were killed; many more were sold as slaves to Tartar merchants who had accompanied him. Towns were set on fire standing crops were destroyed and having stayed here for about eight months Dulucha took about 50,000 Brahmans with himself as slaves only to perish with all his troops and slaves while crossing Devsar pass .Dulucha went away from the country. But his visit had upset the whole social and economic fabric of the country. People were in distress. Lawlessness was rampant, and marauding bands infested the highways. The people had lost all faith in their ruler. All they wanted was a strong man who could establish peace with a resolute will. Such a man they found in Rinchina who had previously repulsed an attack of Khasha tribe where he showed a great deal of military prowess and valor. Without any serious opposition he seized the rule of the country though Ram Chandra the Commander-in-chief of the late king, put in a feeble resistance, but was later defeated and killed. This created not a ripple in the populace anywhere and Rinchina became the undisputed monarch. At that time the roots of Buddhism were getting severed from the Indian nationalism. The supporters of Buddhism had got entangled in inviting foreign invaders to attack India to whom they provided assistance. Since Rinchina was a Buddhist there was need for Indianising his mind and activities. To achieve this, Kotrani agreed to marry Rinchina. Marrying her father's murderer for the welfare of the people of Kashmir, for the protection of the state of Kashmir and for the interest of the nation is a strange and rare example in history. Through the guidance and assistance of Kotrani, Rinchina improved the administrative setup and reorganized the administrative machinery which had been derailed. By changing the outlook of army officers he promoted the feelings of discipline in the Army. He successfully curbed revolts. Kotrani played a pivotal role in giving directions to all these efforts and administrative activities of Rinchina.

Blunder of Brahmins of Tulamula

Through her nature and wisdom Kotrani made Rinchina to accept Hindu religion. Under the influence of Kotarani's opinions, arguments and nationalistic outlook Rinchina decided to join the national mainstream. Kotrani urged him to carry out baptism into Hindu religion through established religious rites and directed him to go to some experienced Pandit at Tulamula. Rinchina went to Tulamula but the then Pundits even being great scholars had lost understanding of the basic elements of religion because of prolonged unrest. As such lacking far sightedness they were incapable of interpreting religion as per the requirements of the era. They straightway refused to initiate Rinchina into Hinduism. Rinchina became angry and annoyed and while reacting to the treatment meted out to him by the Pundits he adopted Islam. Most of his followers and local Buddhist population also embraced Islam. All the patriotic efforts of Kotrani were washed away and the seeds of the cancer of religious conversion were sown. The already available humanitarian outlook and nationalism in Hindu religion were strangled. As a result of this blunder of the then Pundits the cancerous plants are currently emitting fire in Kashmir. Rinchina held the reigns of the Government as a Muslim ruler under the name of Malik Sadruddin. But Kotrani through her sweet behavior managed to restrain his activities to some extent. He succeeded in curbing internal revolts because of Kotarani's clever behavior and political wisdom but he remained ignorant about the conspiracies that were being hatched against him in foreign lands. When Dulucha an invader from central Asia enacted the dance of destruction in Kashmir, King Sahadev had fled and his brother, Udyandev too escaped to Gandhara. After Rinchina assumed power he following his return to Kashmir, attempted to dislodge Rinchina from the seat of power. Udyandev hatched a secret conspiracy with the help of a local influential Sardar. He launched an attack on the palace of Rinchina with the help of his trusted men. Rinchina was injured and a rumor about his death was spread in the entire city. It led to disorder and violence. But peace returned as a result of timely efforts of Kotrani. When Rinchina became fit he, on the imploring of Kotrani, got the rebels killed. However the wounds he had received during an attack on him were so deep that he succumbed to these injuries in 1320 A.D. Just before his death Rinchina summoned his trusted minister Shamir and entrusted his son and wife Kotarani, to his care. This was the same Shah Mir who had come to Kashmir as a religious preacher and who had been appointed as minister by King Sahadev. Rinchina was the first Muslim convert and Shah Mir **first Muslim religious preacher.**

When Rinchina started punishing the rebels, who had attacked him in the palace, Udyandev had managed to escape. He became active again after the death of Rinchina. With the help of an external force he launched an attack on Kashmir. Kashmir was incapable to face this invasion. In the absence of Rinchina no powerful person emerged on the scene. The Army officers too were not united because there was no able commander to guide them. Udyandev started achieving success. Kotrani got worried over the possible fall of Kashmir but she did not give up courage. She was already a diplomat she decided to take necessary steps for the protection of the people which was protection of Kashmir. She thought of one way of putting a nose-ring to Udyandev and that was to marry him for which she sent a proposal to him.

Though Rinchina had established peace, he had not succeeded in curbing totally the anarchic elements. These very anarchic forces raised their head after the death of Rinchina. Kotrani had realized that she could not control the nation with her limited resources and when Udyandev was marching towards Kashmir with a big army the Queen offered herself and her throne to him and discarded the rights of her son Hyder. Udyandev occupied the throne and immediately married Kotrani. Her son Hyder was yet small after the death of Rinchina Hyder had the right to occupy the throne of Kashmir. It was certain that after her marriage with Udyandev Hyder had to lose the throne. But once again Kotrani sacrificed the rights of her son on the altar of Kashmir's interest. Udyandev was simply a twinkling lamp in front of the resplendent glory of Kotrani. With the help of her attraction, beauty and wisdom the queen held Udyandev in her political clutches.

Coward king flees

Kashmir witnessed another powerful invasion. One Turk Tatar Sardar Achalla invaded Kashmir. Udyandev again fled. Udyandev, this time, fled to Tibet following the footsteps of his family. But Kotrani awakened the people of Kashmir about patriotism through her fiery appeal. Thousands of people assembled under the flag of Kotrani and defeated Tatars. To be continued in second week

Kashmir was free of turmoil and danger. Kotarani convened a meeting of all Sardar, Army officials, and politicians, social and religious leaders and told them that if in this hour of national crisis "we do not forget our differences and get united; we may have to face many difficulties". She implored people to remain vigilant about the future while reminding them of the destruction caused during the invasion of Dulucha. People were deeply influenced by her call and they came under one banner in the hour of national crisis after rising above from the group sentiments. Kotarani kept the command of the battle in her hand and the enemy was shaken by the mettle of her sword. Kashmiri Army established its foundation because of her war strategy and Army command. After a battle of a few days the thrust of Achla's Army was stopped. Achla's Army strength was greater than that of the Army in Kashmir. Even while fighting with chivalry Kotarani realized that it was not possible to defeat the foreign invaders because of their bigger number and arms strength. Banking on sound diplomacy she thought of changing the battlefront. In the battlefield fronts have to be changed many a times. One has to adopt a strategy according to the facing enemy. Conspirators should be replied in the language of conspiracy which is considered the best war tactics; annihilate viciousness through wickedness. Kotarani had thrown to winds that policy of liberalism and broadmindedness which was the cause of defeat of the Hindus till now.

Kotarani sent her trusted messenger to Achalla with an offer for truce and informed him that "our troops" were fatigued. She wanted war to be stopped. The ruler of Kashmir had fled out of scare and the throne was vacant. Achalla was told that he could occupy the throne only on one condition that he would withdraw his Army and the fairies of Kashmir would welcome him. And Kotarani would present herself in his service. An expert intriguer in the battlefield and wicked in political behavior Sardar Achalla was ensnared by the sweet words of Kotarani. He sent back all his forces. He started waiting impatiently, along with some colleagues, for Kotarani and for the Kashmiri fairies. He was imagining of being surrounded by fairies. Achalla was engrossed in the imaginary enjoyment of beauty. There and then Kotarani reached there like a roaring lion and with one stroke of her sword beheaded Achalla. The same fate awaited his colleagues. Kotarani emerged victorious. She emerged like Durga in front of the Kashmir's. Senior officers of the administration and the Army and the ministers unanimously declared Kotarani as the Queen of Kashmir.

Here one more important aspect of the character of Kotarani is highlighted. Besides being a cruel battle commander and strong administrator she was also a liberal minded woman. In her person, Indian Woman's devotion and respect for her husband were present. Her husband, Udyandev, had fled leaving her alone during the war. When he came to know that Achalla had been killed and his Army had been defeated and Kotarani had become the Queen of Kashmir, he returned to Kashmir. Kotarani welcomed him and kept him in the palace with honor. She preserved in her the character of an ideal woman. Internal revolt in the state took birth again. Influential groups started emerging on the scene. Internally the embers of revolt started simmering g. She curbed these revolts with her full strength. But she could not completely finish these revolts. Many ministers and Army officers in Kashmir did not like to be governed by a female personality. They tried to dislodge the Queen from the seat of power but every time they had to face defeat.

One a senior Army officer with a company of troops attacked the palace of the Queen. On hearing this news, the Queen, with her security guards, came out to fight the rebel soldiers. But the Army officer succeeded in arresting the Queen. She was imprisoned in a fortress. The Queen had never learnt to be panicky and give up courage. Even while being in the prison she established links with the outside world through her cleverness. She succeeded in escaping from the prison by scaling the wall during the night with the help of her trusted minister, Kumar Bhat. On reaching the capital, she started a terrible military campaign and got killed the rebel officers and their colleagues. All these events were being watched peacefully but with some aim by Shahmir. The purpose for which this Muslim religious preacher had come to Kashmir could not be achieved during the reign of Kotarani. He demonstrated his sound strategy for carving out his way through all these events and dwindling political situation. He earned confidence of Kotarani. He had fully supported Kotarani during her battles with Dulucha and Achalla. He established an honorable place among people and in order to promote family relations with many influential people he organized marriages of the children of his family.

Shahmir started flaring-up Udyandev against the Queen. The Queen's son Hyder, from her first husband, Rinchina, was marching towards maturity. Shahmir told Udyandev that the Queen was making arrangements for installing her son, Hyder, on the throne. This way Hyder will become the King and the son of Udyandev would be thrown out of the state. The

Queen played a trick through which Udyandev was happy and the Shah Mir's dice, which he had thrown, proved a failure. The Queen publicly disowned Rinchina and her son, Hyder, and deprived them of their rights. The Queen had doubts: she thought that since Shahmir had nourished Hyder he (Hyder) will support Shah Mir. Free from worries she started running the state administration. In order to provide justice to the people she made changes in the courts in the state. Those soldiers who had shown their courage and ability in the battle were honored. And those who had played fraud during the war were sacked and punished. She also reorganized her council of ministers. Kotarani was a born administrator. She also started several social reforms' the middle of these tricks Udyandev passed away in 1338 A.D. on the day of Shivratri. In order to prevent rebels from joining hands with Shahmir for usurping the throne of Kashmir, Kotarani kept the news of the death of Udyandev secret for five days. In these five days she took all measures for ensuring security of the state. She deployed her trusted officers on those places which were important from the security point of view. Vigilance was intensified on the border. She appointed one of her close associates, Bhikshan Bhat, as Prime Minister. Within these five days she appointed Lavanya, an influential social leader, as a minister. Both these men were considered the arms of Shahmir. By attracting both of them she almost disabled Shahmir. After the fifth day when the fortification of the state was complete, Kotarani, with the help of her new Prime Minister, Bhikshan Bhat, organized her coronation. Then the news of the death of Udyandev leaked out of the palace. Shahmir kept on repenting. But Shahmir was not silent. He was an expert in hatching conspiracies secretly. He decided to eliminate Prime Minister Bhikshan Bhat by any means because he was the nerve centre of the powers and the rapport with the administrative channels for the Queen. Shahmir had realized that it was not possible to tame this courageous woman neither through revolt nor through love or strength. She had to be eliminated through a simple deceit. The deeds of her fall can be sown by taking advantage of the woman in her and of her liberalism.

Shahmir feigned illness and lay in the bed. Through an employee he sent a message to Kotarani that Shahmir was critically ill and would die. After all Kotarani was a woman and she became upset on hearing about the illness of her one time trusted associate. At once the Queen sent her Prime Minister, Bhikshan Bhat, to enquire about the welfare of Shahmir. Bhikshan Bhat, along with his colleagues and security men, reached the house of Shahmir to enquire about his health. The colleagues and the security men of Bhikshan Bhat were stopped outside the house. The men of Shahmir engaged them in conversation as per the plan. They were told that in view of the health of Shahmir only Bhikshan Bhat could go inside. He went inside and after making enquiries about his health, Shahmir requested him to occupy the seat in front of him. The moment Bhikshan Bhat took the seat, Shahmir immediately wounded him fatally. Bhikshan died on the spot. Kotarani was shocked and enraged on hearing this news but her minister, Lavanya, prevented her from taking revenge at that very moment.

After some time Kamraj area of Kashmir witnessed severe famine. Kotarani's motherly mind cried on seeing people famish. She immediately sent relief and for supervising the relief measures she herself went on tour of the entire area.

When Shahmir came to know that the Queen is away from the capital of Srinagar, he reached Srinagar along with his armed forces. After occupying the city with the help of an Army officer Shahmir declared he the king of the state. Minister, Lavanya, took his trusted men with him and launched an attack on Shahmir. Shahmir was about to be defeated when, on his appeal, many Sardar with their companies of troops reached Srinagar to assist him. Lavanya was surrounded and he had to surrender before the armed strength of Shahmir who took full control of Srinagar.

At that time Kotarani was busy in looking after the relief operations in Kamraj region which had been affected by famine. When the news of occupation of Srinagar by Shahmir reached the Queen, she started collecting her troops at Jaipur (now Andukot), near Kamraj. But already much time had been wasted. By occupying Srinagar Shahmir had become stronger. In order to arrest the Queen, Shahmir set out for the Jaipur fort where Kotarani was formulating the battle strategy.

The Queen was entrapped inside the fort along with her soldiers. Shah Mir's troops cordoned off the entire Fort. The Queen finalized a plan for escaping from the fort after she saw herself having been entrapped but her plan did not fructify because of the alert soldiers of Shahmir. The Queen realized that the end was near; still she did not give up her courage. She decided to play diplomacy and prepared an outline of a scheme for eliminating Shahmir. Kotarani decided to play the last trick of diplomacy of her life. She sent a message to Shahmir offering her the throne and her hand for marriage.

When Shahmir learnt that he was getting both the throne and Kotarani as his wife he gladly accepted the offer. And he invited the Queen to his palace. On receiving Shahmir's invitation, Kotarani was ready to go to him. She dressed and decorated herself fully. She looked like a bride in her lovely attire. Decked in beautiful gold ornaments Kotarani hid a sharp dagger under her garments before moving to the palace. She reached the palace of Shahmir. Shahmir invited her to his bedroom. The moment, the Queen entered into the bedroom she became alert. The Queen had gone inside the bedroom to kill Shahmir with her dagger but the thrust of her dagger proved in vain. The moment Shahmir stepped forward to embrace her; Kotarani ended her life with the same dagger. She did not allow Shahmir to come close to her body.

CHAPTER TWENTY

SHAH MIR(1339-42)

Shah Mir (1339-42)

D

uring the reign of Suhadeva (1301-1320) many Muslim adventurers came to Kashmir. The chief among them was a Muslim missionary- Bulbul Shah. Two others were Shahmir from Swat and Rinchina from Tibet. Shahmir came in AD 1313 along with his numerous relations. Suhadeva granted him a jagir in a village near Baramulla. Ramachandra, the Prime

Minister and Commander-in-Chief of Kashmir, employed Rinchina and granted him jagir in a village in the Lar Valley. These two adventurers were instrumental in the establishment of the Muslim rule in Kashmir. Another adventurer who received Suhadeva's patronage was Lankar Chak. Dulucha, a Tartar chief from Central Asia, invaded Kashmir with 60,000 strong horsemen .In 1339 after defeating Kota Rain by a foul stratagem and procuring her death, Shahmir ascended the throne of Kashmir under the name of Sultan Shamas-ud-Din (The Light of the Religion - Islam). He got khutaba read and the coins struck to his name. Islam became the court religion. Shahmir became the legitimate author and architect of Muslim rule in Kashmir. With the establishment of the new regime Muslim new rule were set for non Muslims

Non Muslims shall not allow fresh constructions of temples and shrines for image worship.

No repair shall be executed to the existing temples and shrines.

They shall not proffer Muslim names.

They shall not ride a harnessed horse.

They shall not move about with arms.

They shall not wear rings with diamonds.

They shall not deal in or eat pig meant

They shall not exhibit idolatrous images.

They shall not built houses in the neighborhood of Muslims.

They shall not dispose of their dead in the neighborhood of Muslim graveyards, nor weep or wail over their dead.

They shall not deal in or buy Muslim slaves.

No Muslim traveler shall be refused lodging in the Hindu temples and shrines where he shall be treated as a guest for three days by non-Muslims.

No non-Muslim shall act as a spy in the Muslim state.

No problem shall be created for those non-Muslims who, of their own will, show their readiness for Islam.

Non-Muslims shall honor Muslims and shall leave their assembly whenever the Muslims enter the premises.

The dress of non-Muslims shall be different from that of Muslims to distinguish themselves.

CHAPTER TWENTY-ONE

SHIHAB-UD-DIN

Shihab-ud-Din (AD 1354-1373)

This naturally caused animosity among the Brahmans and resulted in frail rebellion during the reign of Shihab-ud-Din (AD 1354-1373). In order to break the upheaval among the Hindus and to make them prostrate, the Sultan turned his attention towards their temples. All the temples in Srinagar, including the one at Bijbehara, were wrecked to terrorize the poor Kashmiri Pandits. It seems that by this time, the sultans of Kashmir were perfectly Islamized as a result of their contacts, interactions and intercourses with the sayyids. These sayyids came here as absconders in search of safe harbors', but maneuvered the events for their own cause and fanatic iconoclastic zeal. The Hindus began to feel deserted and alienated in their own land. To consolidate their rule, sultans institutionalized the "policy of extermination" to eradicate all traces of Hinduism in any form. However, the Kashmiri Pandits stuck to their own religion and traditions, ignoring the atrocities, barbarism and cruelties of the privileged ruling class. But there were many from other castes who, either by conviction or in order to gain royal favour, embraced Islam. These new converts were looked down upon by the Kashmiri Pandits as traitorous and treacherous, with no loyalty for time-honored values. This gave rise to a new class rivalry. Suha Bhatt, who after embracing Islam took the name of Saif-ud-Din, became the leader of the fresh converts during the reign of Sikander (AD 1389-1413).

CHAPTER TWENTY-TWO

SIKANDER THE BUTSHIKAN

Sikander the Butshikan (AD 1389-1413).

Sikander the Butshikan was bigoted with fanatic religious zeal to spread Islam in the entire Valley. This fanaticism was stimulated by Mir Muhammad Hamadani. Suha Bhatt - the convert, was appointed Prime Minister by Sikander and both hatched a deadly conspiracy to persecute the Hindus and enforce upon the Nizam-i-Mustafa. The Sultan forgot his kingly duties and took delight day and night in breaking images. He broke images of Martanda, Vishaya, Ishana, Chakrabrit and Tripureshvara. There was no city, no town, no village, and no wood where Turushka left the temples of the gods unbroken. This country possessed from the times of Hindu rajas many temples which were like the wonders of the world. Their workmanship was so fine and delicate that one found himself bewildered at their sight. Sikander, goaded by feelings of bigotry, destroyed them and leveled them with the earth and with the material built many mosques and khanqahs. In the first instance he turned his attention towards the great Martand temple built by Ramdev (the temple was rebuilt by King Lalitaditya, AD 724-760) on Mattan Kareva. For one year he tried to demolish it, but failed. At last in sheer dismay, he dug out stones from its base and having stored enough wood in their place, set fire to it. The gold gilt paintings on its walls were totally destroyed and the walls surrounding its premises were demolished. Its ruins even now strike wonder in men's minds. At Bijbehara, three hundred temples including the famous Vijiveshwara temple, which was partly damaged by Shihab-ud-Din, were destroyed. With the material of Vijiveshwara temple, a mosque was built and on its site at khanqahs, which is even now known as Vijiveshwara Khanqah. The stones and bricks which were once configurated a marvelous and splendid temple or monastery now hold up mosques. Hassan further adds Sikander meted out greatest oppression to the Hindus. It was notified in the Valley that if a Hindu does not become a Muslim, he must leave the country or be killed. As a result some of the Hindus fled away, some accepted Islam and many Brahmans consented to be killed and gave their lives. It is said that Sikander collected, by these methods, six mans of sacred thread form Hindu converts and burnt them. Mir Muhammad Hamadani, who was a witness of all this vicious brutality, barbarism and vandalism, at last advised him to desist from the slaughter of Brahmans and told him to impose jazia (religious tax) instead of death upon them. All the Hindu books of learning were collected and thrown into Dal Lake and were buried beneath stones and earth. Sikander issued orders that no man should wear the Tilak mark on his forehead and no woman be allowed to perform sati.

He also insisted on breaking and melting of all the gold and silver idols of gods and coins the metal into money. An attempt was made to destroy the caste of the Aryan Saraswat Brahmans by force and those who resisted were subject to heavy fines. Many of the Brahmans, rather than abandon their religion or their county, poisoned themselves; some emigrated from their native homes, while a few escaped the evil of banishment by becoming Muhammedans. To strictly enforce the Nizam-i-Mustafa, Sikander established the office of Sheikh-ul-Islam. According to W.R. Lawrence, the Aryan Saraswat Brahmans of Kashmir were given three choices-death, conversion or exile. Many fled, many were converted and many were killed, and it is said that this thorough monarch (Sikander) burnt seven mans s of sacred threads of the murdered Brahmans. As for the statements of Hassan and Lawrence, six mans (37 kg) of sacred threads were burnt of Pandits of who were either murdered or converted Pandits. The number of people, to whom these thirteen mans of sacred threads belonged, might have been big number. A mammoth number of the Saraswat Pandits also went into exile, causing the first disastrous mass exodus of the community

CHAPTER TWENTY-THREE

LAL DED (1320-1392)

Lal Ded (1320–1392)

Lal Ded known as Laleshwari was a Kashmiri mystic of the Kashmir Shaivism School of philosophy. She was the creator of the style of mystic poetry called Vakhs, literally speech (from Sanskrit vaak). Known as Lal Vakhs, her verses are the earliest compositions in the Kashmiri language and are an important part in the history of modern Kashmiri literature. Lal Ded is bold yet honest an introduction of woman who had the courage to break away from a society defined by orthodoxy and prejudice and bridge the gap between faiths and gender. Lal Ded is today celebrated as a literary great, who defined the modern-day Kashmiri language, but for generations of Kashmiri, she is a spiritual figure whose Vakhs (verses or sayings) have been revered for nearly 700 years. Lal Ded is equally admired by Hindus and Muslims, who refer to her as Laleshwari and Lalla Arifa, respectively. In 1320, the country was attacked by Zulchu, a Central-Asian chieftain, which led to the downfall of the last Hindu king of Kashmir, Sahadeva. Zulchu is said to have massacred thousands of locals and also forced them to convert to Islam. Once he left, the kingdom was in disarray .Lal Ded grew up in these turbulent times and we can get a glimpse of her life story from her Vakhs. After her primary education, she was married at the age of 12, and given a new name Padmavati as was the norm then. However, it wasn't a very happy marriage, with her mother-in-law constantly mistreating her. Lal Ded was starved was by her mother in law. Her mother-in-law put a stone in her plate and then covered it with a thin layer of rice, so that it appeared to outsiders that she had been served a heap of rice. Lal Ded found little sympathy in her husband, who was blinded by his mother's accusations against her, including claims that she was cheating on him. His mother had arrived at this conclusion because, every morning, Lal Ded left the house to fill a pot of water from the river and returned only in the evening. What her mother-in-law didn't know was that, in-between; Lul Ded was spending time at a Shiva temple on the other side of the river. Lal Ded was an ardent devotee. All in all, it was a miserable life and instead of bearing it all like numerous other young girls of her time did Lal Ded walked out. Lal Ded became a wandering mendicant. She also disrobed herself, a sign that she wanted to leave behind the unnecessary baggage of culture and clothing and look forward to dwelling upon the inner self. By now considered a mad mystic due to her actions, she roamed naked, reciting her Vakhs.

Lal Ded's Vakhs are among the earliest known manifestations of Kashmiri literature. In fact, it was her work that laid the foundation of the modern Kashmiri language. Lal Ded was a rebel and rejected conventional society and attacked its rituals. She was also critical of religious orthodoxy. Her Vakhs have underlying thoughts of defiance. Lal Ded died in her 70s. Sufis missionaries utilized her Hindu philosophy.Laleshwari locally popular as Lal Ded, was a Kashmiri mystic of the early medieval period, renowned for her devotional lyrical verse. Her spiritualist compositions, musings, methods and practices were universal, holistic and transcendental in appeal, and thus inspired Hindus and Muslims alike. She managed to express insight in brevity, simplicity and above all generality, surpassing most of her comparatively narrow minded contemporaries. She emphasized sentimental abstraction and was a pioneering, vocal critic of superficialities as idolatry. She was instrumental to the body of vernacular mysticism in the region, and a harmonizing influence and crucial link between traditional mysticism, the popular Bhakti movement and Sufism.

Her various works were analyzed and retold more poetically from an Islamic perspective. Sufi retellings, not only adapted but embellished her works to cater to abstract Islamic sensibilities, rendering them more concise, artistic and poetic in nature. The introduction of these subtle alterations helped capture popular imagination and summit Lal Ded's legacy as an omnipresent, transcendental, cultural figure. The unique, simple-devotional character of her Salhana helped enable spiritualism as commonplace and household, for posterity. By ridding Shaivism of customary ritualism's and fringe practices, she made it readily accessible and universal in appeal. Her practice replaced esotericism with devout emotion. While Lal Ded was stylized independently and varyingly by each community, she was simultaneously co-existed as the Lalla Yogini to the Hindus and the Lalla Arifa to the Muslims; but both affectionately referred to her as Lal Ded. That precisely makes it all the more grave a misfortune that in contemporary reality, these connotations are increasingly inter competing and undoing the very inherent underlying unity of spiritualism that Lal Ded strived to expose. Her single greatest prowess lay in being able to broad mindedly entertain any depiction, portrayal and attribute ascribed to the formless deity, and visualizing the abstract Almighty in every deed and manifestation.

CHAPTER TWENTY-FOUR

ALI SHAH (1413-30 AD)

Ali Shah (AD 1413-1430)

Ali Shah son of Sikander the Butshikan, during his short rule of six years, carried on his father's 24-year tyrant reign with homicides, conversions, tyranny and enforced jazia. Suha Bhatta the convert, who retained the prime minister ship, continued his earlier crimes and atrocities against the Kashmiri Pandits. Jonaraja gives a graphic account of the plight of the illustrious Kashmiri Pandits in the draconian reign of Ali Shah. He says Suha Bhatta the convert, passed the limit by levying fine, jazia, on the twice born. This evil-minded man forbade ceremonies and processions on the new moon. He became envious that the Brahmans who had become fearless would keep up their caste by going over to foreign countries, he therefore ordered posting of squads on the roads, not to allow passage to any one without a passport. Then as the fisherman torments fish, so this low born man tormented the twice-born in this country. The legendary Brahmans burnt themselves in the flaming fire through fear of conversion. Some Brahmans killed themselves by taking poison, some by the rope and others by drowning themselves. The country was contaminated by hatred and the king's favorites could not prevent one in a thousand from committing suicide. A multitude of celebrated Brahmans, who prided in their caste, fled from the country through bye-roads as the main roads were closed. Even as men depart from this world, so did the Aryan Saraswat Brahmans of Kashmir flee to foreign countries. The difficult countries through which they passed, the scanty food, painful illness and the torments of hell during life time removed from the minds of the Kashmiri Pandits the fears of hell. Oppressed by various calamities such as encounter with the enemy, fear of snakes, fierce heat and scanty food; many Brahmans perished on the way and thus obtained salvation." This was the second miserable mass exodus of the Kashmiri Pandits.

CHAPTER TWENTY-FIVE

SULTAN ZAIN -UL-ABIDIN

Sultan Zain-ul-Abidin (1420 to 1470)

Zain-ul-Abidin was the second and the most favorite son of Sultan Sikander but was unlike his father in many ways. The period of his father is remembered for persecution of Brahmans, a large number of who had migrated from Kashmir. On ascending the throne of Kashmir, Zain-ul-Abidin found the whole country in chaos. . The first and foremost task for him was to bring some order to chaotic conditions. For this he motivated the old class of officials, the Pandits, to return to Kashmir giving them every facility and guaranteeing them religious and civil liberties. The King severely dealt with all corrupt officials to ensure corruption was completely rooted out. He dealt ruthlessly with all types of crime and most of the known criminals were put behind the bars. Zain-ul-Abidin's first great reform was the revision of land assessment. He reduced it to a fourth of the total produce in some places and to a seventh in others. Sultan was a great builder. Remains of his numerous towns, villages, canals, and bridges still exist and bear his name. To increase agricultural production, he utilized the fertile but dry soil of the karewas for which purpose he built numerous canals such as Utpalapur, Nandashaila, Bijbehara, Advin, Amburher, Manasbal, Zainagir, and Shahkul at Bawan. This gave a tremendous boost to agricultural production in the valley. He built many bridges including the first wooden bridge in Srinagar still known as Zainakadal (now replaced by a concrete bridge). One of his engineers, Damara Kach constructed a paved road which could be used even in rains. Sultan was very fond of wooden architecture and built the palaces of Rajdan and Zain Dab in Zainagiri. These were very beautiful and artistic buildings. The former was twelve storeys high with numerous rooms, halls, verandas, and staircases. The latter was burnt down by chaks. He also built rest houses for travelers and laid many beautiful gardens, prominent being Baghi Zainagiri, Baghi Zaina Dab, Baghi Zainpur, and Baghi Zainakut. The layout of these gardens depicted influences from Samarqand and Bukhara. Zain-ul-Abidin had great love for learning, music, and dance. After ascending the throne, he invited a large number of competent teachers and craftsmen from Samarqand to train his subjects in these arts. Some of the handicrafts introduced include carpet weaving, papier mache, silk, paper making etc. Kashmiri artisans improved and perfected these arts to such a level that their fame spread to whole Asia and even to Europe. Towards the end of his reign a very severe famine occurred in Kashmir. This was caused by an early snowfall which destroyed the fully ripe paddy crop. Unfortunately the succeeding winter was also very severe. A large number of people died. The King made all out efforts to alleviate the suffering of the people.

CHAPTER TWENTY-SIX

PANDIT SHRIYA BHAT

Pandit Shriya Bhat

Shriya Bhatt belonged to a family of Vaids or practitioners of Ayurvedic system of medicine Shriya Bhatt's family was witness to the death and destruction brought upon in Kashmir .The state of Kashmir had become almost Hindu less because of the massive and powerful campaign for religious conversion launched by Sikander and his son, cruel Ali Shah. Only a few Hindu families were living in Kashmir after paying taxes and after tolerating many difficulties and ignominies. The cries of the raped Hindu women were reverberating in Kashmir. The silence of the ruins of the temples was generating terror. The water of the Jhelum was still red with the blood of the Kashmiri Hindus. In this dark a ray hope as a result of efforts of Sultan Zainulab-ud-Din and Pandit Shri Bhat the ancient glory of Kashmir started returning. Temples started being built, ban was imposed on slaughter of cows, taxes were abolished and the migrant Hindus returned to their houses.

In year 1420 A.D. Sikander's second son, Sultan Zainulab-ud-Din, occupied the throne of Kashmir. He decided to compensate for the cruel activities and the sin of his father. Zainulab-ud-Din tried to turn Kashmir towards its ancient glory. Under his orders many ruined temples were rebuilt. Those Kashmiri Pandits, who had migrated and scattered in different areas in India were invited back. Many industries were set up for the welfare of the people. Barren lands were made cultivable. For improving irrigation many plans were introduced. Constructive minded Sultan Zainulab-ud-Din, started many schemes for promoting art and culture. He got many Hindu scriptures translated in Persian .Behind all this good work and his awakened sympathy towards all human beings is hidden one important event, which the historians have concealed, which pertains to the change of his mind brought about by Pandit Shriya Bhat.

Sultan Zainulab-ud-Din had hardly completed two years on the throne when a dangerous boil developed on his chest. Many Syed Hakims treated him. Known Hakims from Central Asia came to treat him but there was no improvement. Sultan l had heard that there was Hindu Vaid in Kashmir who had the expertise in curing the boil. Under the orders of the Sultan a search launched for such Vaid. Ultimately Government employees found Shriya Bhat, an expert in treating poisonous boils. .

When the Sultan was fully well, he wanted to reward Shriya Bhat with jewels and diamonds but Shriya Bhat refused to accept any such regard. He did not bother about his personal comforts and amenities. He gave preference to the happiness and prosperity of his Kashmir. This attitude of Shriya Bhat was something new for the Sultan. By rejecting wealth and prosperity Shriya Bhat, while thinking in terms of the benefit of the nation, had decided to make the King adopt a liberal outlook and transform his lifestyle in the background of the historical and constructive mould. The Sultan witnessed transformation in the outlook of life and his religious fervor ended giving place to broadmindedness instead of narrow-mindedness.

On being told by the Sultan Shri Bhat submitted seven demands which Sultan Zainulab-ud-Din, accepted gladly. These demands were:

1. The massacre of Hindus on the basis of religious conflict is to be stopped immediately and no one be punished without proper investigations and enquiries.

2. Those temples, which were damaged during the time of his father and brother to be rebuilt. Permission is given to those Hindus, who had been forcibly converted to Islam, to return to the religion of their ancestors. Those Kashmiri who had migrated out of fear to areas outside Kashmir, where they were leading a life of penury, be immediately invited back to their houses.

3. The taxes imposed and the ban on performing Yagniya and rites and customs of Hindus be lifted on the Hindus be abolished and they be given equal rights.

History is witness to the fact that the Sultan accepted all the demands submitted by the patriot, Shriya Bhat .Sanskrit scholars, who had migrated from the valley, returned to Kashmir and again Kashmiri Pandit families started resettling in Kashmir. On the request of Shri Bhat the Government sanctioned monetary help to the students and the scholars and many Sanskrit centers were reopened. The property of Hindus looted during the period of Sikander was returned to them. Sultan Zainulab-ud-Din developed faith in Hindu religion. He started the study of Hindu scriptures. .Because of the efforts of Shriya Bhat when Hindu families returned to Kashmir for resettlement, the problem of their houses and earning cropped up. Under the guidance of Shri Bhat and under the permission and plan of the Government everyone was appointed on different posts in the Government as per their caliber. Shriya Bhat resolved successfully all the problems connected with their resettlement, their family arrangements, their security and their identity while linking them with the then administrative setup. Shriya Bhat has, through his revolutionary reforms, organized a classless and one class society not only in the history of Kashmir but for the entire Hindu society of India, on the scientific lines, while looking a thousand years ahead of him. It is surprising that the reforms for which Bhakti revolution, Brahma Samaj and Arya Samaj wanted to implement the bugle of this reform was sounded several hundred years ago by Shri Bhat in 1420 A.D. It was an instance of his deep insight in future .Because of his unique and lovely personality he had not only influenced the Sultan but had also attracted him. He had eclipsed the biased influenced of Muslim ministers who had come from central Asia by his extraordinary personality.

CHAPTER TWENTY-SEVEN

NUDRISHI(Sheikh Nur-Ud-Din)

Nund Rishi (1377 – 1438 AD)

Noor-ud-Din was born in modern-day village Qaimoh in Kulgam district in 1377 AD to Salar Sanz and Sadra, also called Sadra Moji or Sadra Deddi. His grandfather Sheikh Salah-Ud-Din hailed from Kisthwar. The legend has it that he refused to be breast-fed by his mother after birth and it was Laleshwari who breastfed him. In teenage years Noor-ud-Din was apprenticed to a couple of traders. He was probably married to Zia Ded who hailed from the village of Dadasara, Tral and had two sons and a daughter with her. Noor-ud-Din renounced the worldly life at the age of 30 and retired to live a life of meditation in a cave which is still shown in Qaimoh and is about 10 feet deep. During his last days, he survived by drinking a cup of milk every day, and later, he used to survive by drinking water.

The great sage was one of the twin stars of medieval Kashmir along with Laleshwari (Lul Ded) with whom he shared the intensity of mystic experience whose profundity remains unrivalled to this day. A Kashmiri poetess Lul Ded was his contemporary and had a great impact on his spiritual growth. Some scholars argue that he was her disciple, and associate his poetry with the Bhakti movement, although others disagree .There has been a galaxy of Muslim saints and sages and some great ones among them commanded the respect and allegiance of vast numbers of Hindus also. But they have not been known by Hindu names among their non-Muslim followers. Sheikh Nur-ud-Din alone enjoyed this rare distinction.

According to the known facts of his life, but what he saw going on around him made him intensely sad, and he lost interest in life as norm disgusted with the ways of the world, and deciding upon renunciation, retired to caves for meditation at the age of thirty and lived for twelve years in wilderness. So he took to caves and solitary places for severe penance and meditation. In addition to leading a retired life, he was one of those who continually fast. Like Hindus .He had given up eating meat and onions.

He seems to have realized that Kashmir's' precious heritage, so dear to him, which was sought to be destroyed by outsiders, could be saved only by a happy marriage of the best in the old and the new, in the union of the Hindus and the Muslims into a common brotherhood, in their co-existence and cooperation and not in confrontation. That is why he again calls upon the people, especially those who came from outside and the zealots among the new converts, to live together in unison, so that God Himself would rejoice. He called upon them to subdue the five senses, and get over the evils of Kama, Krodha, Lobha, Moha and Ahankara to achieve the highest to make union with Shiva (as he puts it) reminding them that mere lowering of the fleshy body would not save them. He calls upon the people not to go to priests and Mullahs, not to shut themselves up in places of worship or forests but to enter their own body with breath controlled, in communion with God. Again and again he stresses the need for unity among Hindus and Muslims; God Himself would rejoice, he adds, if this happy consummation came about. It was for views such as these that Sheikh- ul-Alam came to be designated Alamdar or standard-bearer of Kashmir.

We know it from the contemporary historian, Jonaraja, that Mala Nurdin, as he calls him, was imprisoned and put under restraint during Ali Shah's time. And Amin Kamil tells us how the Rishinamas reveal that outsiders were opposed to him and harassed him in many ways. But little daunted, he pursued his enlightened course, as though to justify his title to being called Alamdar of Kashmir and all that it had stood for at its best.

The Sheikh's spiritual eminence and his humanistic philosophy made him the idol of the people of Kashmir. They flocked to him and some of them modeled their very lives on his pattern. These latter who came to be known as Rishis, after him, were of great help and assistance to him in the stupendous task that he had undertaken .Rishis were by no means new to Kashmir.

Literary works

Noor-ud-Din spread his teachings or message through poems, commonly known as shruks. His poems have four to six lines each and evolve around religious themes, highlight moral principles and often call for peace. He strived for Hindu Muslim unity. One of his prominent poems is Ann poshi teli yeli wan poshi, which translates as Food will thrive only till the woods survive.Noor-ud-Din died in 1438 at the approximate age of 63. Sultan Zain-ul-Abidin commissioned a tomb for his body at Charar-e-Sharief. The Charar-e-Sharief shrine is visited by pilgrims to this day, especially on the eve of Noor-ud-Din's birth anniversary .The Afghan governor Atta Muhammad Khan minted coins with Noor-ud-Din's name.

CHAPTER TWENTY-EIGHT

MIR SHAMA-UD-DIN IRAQI

Mir Shams-ud-Din Iraqi

Mir Shams-ud-Din Iraqi, who visited the Saffron Valley twice in AD 1477 and 1496, was the founder of Nurbakhshiya order (Shia sect) in Kashmir. His mission was the vigorous propagation of his faith. So, not contented with peaceful preaching's violent methods were employed. In this adventure, Iraqi was helped by the homicidal creature and most dreaded tyrant- Malik Musa Raina, a convertee, whose original name was Soma Chandra. Not only the poor vulnerable Brahmans, but the Sunni Muslims were also violently converted to Shia sect by murderous techniques. This dogmatic fanaticism even crippled the Sunni ruler of

Kashmir, Fateh Shah (1510-1517). A Khanqah was built at Zadibal (Srinagar) by Iraqi, which became the nucleus of Shia concentration. Kashmiri Pandits suffered ferociously under the instructions of Shams-ud-Din Iraqi and Musa Raina. About 24,000 of them were forcibly converted to Shia sect of Islam. Iraqi had even issued orders that everyday about 1500 to 2000 Brahmans be brought to his doorsteps, remove their sacred threads, administer Kalima to them, circumcise them and make them eat beef. These decrees were ferociously and brutally carried out. The Hindu religious scriptures from 7th century AD onwards and about 18 magnificent temples were destroyed, property confiscated and ladies abused. Thousands of Brahmans killed themselves to evade this horrific barbarism and thousands migrated to other places, resulting in their third tragic mass exodus from the Saffron Valley of Kashmir. Those who stayed behind were not only forced to pay jazia, but their noses and ears were chopped off.

CHAPTER TWENTY-NINE

YUSUF SHAH CHAK

Yusuf Shah Chak

Gazi Chak laid the foundation of the Chak Dynasty. The Chak rule began in 1561 and lasted till 1587, when the Mughal emperor, Jalal-Ud-Din Akbar arrested Yusuf shah Chak by trick. Before that undaunted, the young king, however, rose to the occasion, when in 1586, the Mughal launched a full-scale attack on Kashmir. Yusuf Shah offered stiff resistance to the invading armies. A bloody battle followed, but the Mughal armies, although superior in numbers and highly skilled in the art of war, could not subdue the brave Kashmiri who had rallied behind their king to beat back the invaders. Finding that the going was tough and that war could not help them, the Mughal thought of a trick to achieve their objective. They invited Yusuf Shah to come to the Imperial Court at Agra for peace talks. Ignoring the advice of his ministers and commanders to the contrary, the young king, with a view to sparing his people from suffering caused by a devastating war, accepted the invitation and went to Agra, never to return to his native land. Akbar imprisoned him and held him in captivity until December 1587. Subsequently, Yusuf Shah was exiled to Bihar and given a jagir in Biswas. Later, the Mughals compelled him to accompany their army, which conquered Orissa in 1592. And there at Jagatnath Puri, he, the Sultan of Kashmir, died on September 22, 1592. His body was carried to Biswak where it was ultimately buried on interned on 25th of December 1592.

He was expert in the science of music, fond of Persian and Kashmiri poetry, patron of poets, scholars and musicians and himself a poet, Yusuf Shah was one of the most cultured rulers of that period. Though not possessed of any personal velour, he displayed, when he first ascended the throne, promptness and energy in suppressing the revolt of his uncle Abdul Chak. On being driven out of Kashmir, he again displayed enterprise and initiative in his attempts to recover the throne. After regaining the kingdom, he tried to promote the welfare of his people. He prohibited the soldiers from taking unpaid labor from the peasants and unlike his predecessors; he gave up the practice of extracting unpaid labor and Zakat from the hanjis. He also abolished Jaziya and taxes of an oppressive nature cattle and artisans. Yusuf Shah holds a unique place in the cultural history of Kashmir. He was a romantic figure whose life resembles a classic tragedy more than one sense. When Yusuf Shah Chak was taken to the court of Emperor Akbar, he (Akbar) became quite fond of him for his love of music. Such was the depth of Yusuf Shah's knowledge of music, that once when the great Tansen was striking a wrong note while singing Rag Kalawant, he at once pointed out the mistake to the singer, who promptly acknowledged hid superior knowledge and corrected himself. He missed the society of poets, scholars and musicians but above all, he pined for his beloved queen, Habba Khatoon. She was the daughter of a peasant of the village of Chandahar. She had been unhappy with her first husband who were a drunkard and a debauchee and who ill-treated her. A poetess and a musician, possessed a sweet voice, she captivated the heart of Yusuf Shah who fell in love with her and married her. He built for her mountain resorts in Gulmarg, Sonarmarg and other beautiful spots.

Yaqub Shah ascended the throne in 1586 when his father (Yusuf Shah) was imprisoned by the blood thirty Akbar by the trick. He was a great ruler and well wisher of his kingdom, Yaqub shah gave special status to minorities during his reign. Yaqub Shah is known as the last independent ruler of Kashmir. Yokub carried on warfare against the Mughal Empire but surrendered to Akbar on 8 August 1589 a Yaqub Shah died in 1593. He was believed to have been poisoned.

CHAPTER THIRTY

HABA KHATOON

Habba Khatoon

In Kashmir there were many women poets from all manner of social and linguistic backgrounds who dared to be heard and more importantly, considered their voices worth hearing. In 16th century Kashmir, one such woman was Habba Khatoon.It tells a heart-wrenching story of a blooming romance between a courtesan and the prince, and how it was put to an end at the orders of the emperor. Although the veracity of this tale is doubtful, like all legends, it survives and is retold. However, this is not the only romance that Akbar put a premature end to. There is yet another epic, often told and retold in Kashmiri folklore, which does not find mention in popular narratives.

Habba Khatoon, named Zoon (meaning moon) by her parents, was a Kashmiri poetess in the 16th century. Yusuf Shah Chak, the king of Kashmir, spotted her in the fields one day. Legend has it that he fell in love with the beauty of her voice and richness of her rhyme. He is said to have relieved her of her earlier marriage and taken her away to his court, where she enchanted him with her poetry, while reigning as queen for six years. At the end of those six years, Akbar summoned Yusuf Shah to Delhi. Akbar had failed to conquer Kashmir militarily and now resorted to tactics of cozenage. Upon reaching the Mughal court, Yusuf Shah was flung into prison, never to see the light of day again, and never to see his beloved Habba again. For the rest of her years, Habba pined away in an abode next to the Jhelum, where she finally lay to rest. There exists little documentation and fewer records of the story of Habba Khatoon and Yusuf Shah Chak, yet this story has been passed down for generations and it slowly, yet inevitably, found its way into historical records and books of lore.

It is not only her tale but also her verse that has travelled across time to be alive and loud. The clichéd line, Nightingale of Kashmir, has often been used to describe her. She is the sound and song of many gatherings even today. Looking carefully at her context, Habba Keaton's verses are surprisingly bold. That she recited them in the 16th century make her words even more powerful. She did not fit into the existing lineage of women poets before and immediately after her, many of who wrote of spirituality and mysticism. She, on the other hand, brought in a romantic lyricism to Kashmiri.One can even retell her story through her verse her poetry is biographical but also has an inherent universality, much like this verse

Habba articulated her lived reality in verse, yet what makes her stand out is not only the extraordinariness of her life as a peasant-queen-poetess, but the articulation of desire in words that were thus far limited to men. Habba dared to name and beckon her lover, a significant role-reversal at a time when women were only the objects of desire only especially

The reliability in her verse didn't stop at descriptions of conjugal love. Habba lent her voice to the banal chores of everyday life; singing as she went along. It is no wonder then that her verses gained widespread popularity in the region. She wrote of miseries inflicted upon her by her in laws and of the perils of physical labor. Her descriptors of sweat and toil are also beautifully poetic. Much of her poetry is rooted in the flora of

Kashmir: descriptors of hills and streams, flowers and fruits that lend a truly paradisiacal quality to the Kashmir she describes.

While we cannot be certain that she was the only woman poet of her time, she was certainly the first to usher in a lyrical age of romantic poetry in the memory of Kashmiri literature. Her successor in this genre would not show up until two centuries later in the form of poetess Arnimal.Of the repertoire of songs and poems in her name, scholars say; only a handful can be indubitably attributed to Habba. Her position and her story made her worthy of memorializing .Passed down orally in songs that have been sung by women across centuries, it is likely that Habba's words have been modified, reinterpreted and remained by many other unnamed voices. All these voices may have eventually contributed to the myth and legend of Habba Khatoon. Given the universal reliability of her verse, it would not be surprising if Habba's voice has carried the ideas of many lyrically gifted women of Kashmir since. Habba has been a subject of fascination, be this very early film or Muzaffar Ali's attempt to recreate her story on the Hindi film screen. In Kashmir, a recent surge in reinventing old Kashmiri music as pop is a trend and many contemporary musicians, often men, have put Habba's songs in verse and lending their voice to it

CHAPTER THIRTY-ONE

MUGHAL RULE IN KASHMIR(1580-1750 AD)

Mughal rule in Kashmir (1580s–1750s)

Kashmir did not witness direct Mughal rule till the reign of Mughal Akbar, who visited the valley himself in 1589 AD. The Mughal conquered Kashmir and added it in 1586 to his Afghan province Kabul Subah, but Shah Jahan carved it out as a separate subah (imperial top-level province), with seat at Srinagar. During successive Mughal emperors many celebrated gardens, mosques and palaces were constructed. Jahangir and Shah Jahan were not so tolerant. But their religious enthusiasm cannot be termed as fanatic. During this period, the Brahmans could perform their religious ceremonies after paying some tribute. But the whole scenario changed with the accession of Aurangzeb to the throne.

Jahangir, Akbar's son made a departure from the path of religious tolerance and non-interference in other religious affairs. His sectarian predilection and prejudices were clearly pronounced. He shuffled his stances in his dealing with Kashmiri Pandits and his inconsistencies were to a large extent responsible for the communal frenzy and rioting to resurface in its full fury. It was during his rule the Kashmiri Pandits were forced to marry their daughters to Mughal officers and Subedar's .He upheld and followed in letter and spirit Islamic practices. This blots and besmears his image of being a tolerant ruler. He disapproved of and opposed matrimonial relations between Hindus and Muslims but declared that while a Hindu was forbidden by law to marry a Muslim woman. Muslim had the license to marry a Hindu woman.

Jahangir did not lag behind in following the footprints of earlier Muslim fanatics. It was at his behalf that the flight of steps linking the temple of Shankeracharya to the river Jhelum near the temple of Trepursundary was dismantled and the smooth chiseled stones thus got were used by Noorjehan to erect the massive mosque at Pather Masjid in down town Srinagar on the west bank of over Jhelum. The Mughal Sardar Itquad Khan, cruel and inhuman as he was, further tarnished and blackened Jahangir's image that had already been spoiled by anti-Hindu pursuits in Kashmir. Itquad Khan forced the Hindus at gun point to get converted to Islam and tortured them by levying taxes on them. As the Shia Chaks had persecuted Sunni Muslims, he persecuted the Shias.

ShahJehan was a chip of the old block of his father and proved true to him. No less ardent lover and admirer of the natural beauty of Kashmir he did conceal the ugliness in his mind. He did justice to his faith as a Muslim in devoting himself to torturing and persecuting the Kashmiri Hindu.

ShahJehan did not fall to keep up the iconoclastic heritage of his father and did his bit by desecrating and demolishing a number of temples in Kashmir. Bernier is reliable in his conclusive finding that the doors and pillars were found in some of the idol temples demolished by ShahJehan and it is impossible to estimate their value. ShahJehan showed his love for gardens by laying out Shalimar, Nishat, and Achabal. He also got constructed many mosques, but hardly cared to reconstruct temples, monasteries and libraries of Hindus demolished and destroyed by Islamic zealots preceding him.

With his bigoted fanatic and dogmatic approach, the Kashmiri Pandits were once again made vulnerable. Iftikar Khan, the Mughal governor of Kashmir during the reign of Aurangzeb, brutally tyrannized over the Brahmans to such an extent that they approached Guru Teg Bhahadur, the ninth Sikh Guru, at Anandpur in Punjab and solicited his personal intervention with the Emperor. This ultimately led to the Guru's martyrdom and made Guru Gobind Singh to create the Khalsa to fight the oppressors. Muzaffer Khan, Nassar Khan and Ibrahim Khan were other governors of Aurangzeb who ferociously terrorized the Kashmiri Pandits. These celebrated scapegoats were once again forced to migrate from the land of their origin. It was the fourth disastrous mass exodus of the Aryan Saraswat Brahmans from Kashmir.

Aurangzeb whose life is a sharp contrast to that of his predecessors/ ancestors lost no time after ascending the throne in Delhi in 1658 to convert whole of India to Islam.During the latter part of his rule Kashmir witnessed the outbreak of the worst kind of religious intolerance. In AD 1720, Mullah Abdul Nabi, also called Muhat Khan, a non-resident Kashmiri Muslim, was appointed as Shaikhul Islam. In order to assert his religious authority, he asked the Deputy Governor, Mir Ahmed Khan, to start a campaign of persecution of the Kafirs (infidels) - as the Kashmiri Pandits were called. In order to satisfy his satanic ego, the Mulla issued six commandments:

1. No Hindu should not ride a horse, nor should a Hindu wear a shoe;
2. That they should not wear Jama (Mughal costume);
3. That they should move bear arms;
4. That they should not visit any garden;
5. That they should not have Tilak mark on their foreheads;
6. That their children should not receive any education.

But Ahmed Khan refused to execute the mischievous decree. The Mullah then excited his followers against the Kashmiri Pandits. He established his seat in a mosque, assumed the duties of the administrator under the title of Dindar Khan and let loose the reign of terror. The Hindus were wickedly tormented, their houses burnt and property looted. Hundreds of Brahmans were killed, prostrated, maimed and humiliated. They began to run away in large numbers and hide themselves in mountainous terrain. This was the fifth dreadful mass exodus of the legendary Kashmiri Pandits from their mystic motherland. Those who remained behind lived in the most horrific and terrible conditions generated by the Mullah and his gang.

CHAPTER THIRTY-TWO

AFGHAN RULE IN KASHMIR (1750-1819)

Afghan rulers (1750s–1819)

After Aurangzeb's death, the decline of Mughal power Ahmad Shah Abdali conquered it in 1752. The Afghans ruled it till 1819. As long as they got their annual tribute of Rs 20 lakhs a year, the Afghan king did not interfere in the administration. There were 28 governors during Afghan rule of which there was only one Hindu, Sukhjiwan.In 1753, he was the first Hindu chief of Kashmir since 1320 i.e., in 433 years. He was a brave soldier, wise administrator, scholar and poet. His liberal and sympathetic outlook won the hearts of all. He revolted against the Ahmad Shah Abdali who invaded Kashmir with the help of Ranjit Deo, the ruler of Jammu. Sukhjiwan.In was captured, blinded and trampled to death by horses. After this Afghan rule was a tale of atrocities. Sunni - Shia riots broke out in 1763-65. It was a period of cruelty, homicide and anarchy. W.R. Lawrence calls it the reign of brutal tyranny. The barbarous Afghans employed every wild, inhuman, primitive, ferocious, cruel and brutal method to suppress the Kashmiri Brahmans. A pitcher filled with ordure was placed on the head of a Pandit and stones were pelt on it, till it broke and the unfortunate Brahman become wet with filth. Their brutality and atrocity crossed the extreme limits when Hindus were tied up in grass sacks, two and two, and drowned in the Dal Lake. The victimized Hindu was forced to flee the country or were killed or converted to Islam. There was horrible mass exodus of the Kashmiri Pandits, sixth one, to faraway places like Delhi, Allahabad, etc. Many covered the long distances on foot. Hindu parents destroyed the beauty of their daughters by shaving their heads or cutting their noses and ears to save them from degradation. Any Muslim could jump on the back of a Pandit and take a ride. Mir Hazar an Afghan governor, used leather bags instead of grass sacks for the drowning of Brahmans. Turbans and shoes were forbidden for them. The Saraswat Brahmans of Kashmir were also forced to grow beards and Tilak was interdicted. The Afghans are now only remembered for their barbarity, brutality, ferocity, tyranny and cruelty. They thought no more of cutting of heads than of plucking a flower. Ata M. K. Alkozai forcibly seized pretty girls to satisfy his lust. Many parents were forced to shave the heads of their daughters rather than allow them to be molested and degraded. This forced many Pandit families to migrate to Rajauri, Poonch and Delhi. As a result of oppression, great unrest spread in the province. It was conquered by Maharaj Ranjit Singh in 1819

CHAPTER THIRTY-THREE

MATA RUPA BHAWANI(1621-1721)

Mata Rupa Bhawani (1621 – 1721 AD)

Rupa Bhawani was the great mystic poet of 17th century. She had a great and deep experience of ups and downs of life. The worldly sufferings showed her the path of spiritual life. Her Guru was her father Pandit Madhav Jo Dhar who initiated her into the mysteries and practices of yoga. She gave rich mystic poetry to Kashmiri language. In her poetry, we can find the influence of both Kashmir Shaivism and Islamic Sufism. This great mystic poetess had experienced the truth and then explained the same. Such mystics had real experience and not a bookish one. That is the reason why this mystic poetry in every language is considered great after so many centuries.

In the early seventeenth century, a Kashmiri Pundit named Madhav Jo Dhar lived in Srinagar. Madhav Jo was of a deeply religious and philosophical temperament, and his daily life was conducted in an impeccably religious spirit. He worshipped the Supreme Being (Ishwara) in the form of the Divine Mother Sharika (Durga).In Srinagar, there is a hill known as Hara Parvat or Sharika Parvat where the Goddess Sharika is worshipped since ancient times. In 1621, in the month of Jyeshtha, on the Poornima Tithi (full moon), in the early morning a daughter was born to Madhav Jo's wife. He named his daughter Alakshyeshvari, which means one who is imperceptible and indescribable

In her father's house, Alakshyeshvari years of childhood were passed in the company of devotees. Madhav Jo was held in high esteem, and spiritual seekers came from far-away provinces to meet him. Alakshyeshvari spirituality blossomed early in these favorable conditions. As she grew older, the spiritual tendencies within her became increasingly manifest. Her father, Madhav Jo, himself became her guru and gave her spiritual initiation. Nevertheless, in accordance with the prevailing customs of the time, her father arranged her marriage to a young man of the nearby Sapru family .However Alakshyeshvari married life was unhappy. Her husband, Hiranand Sapru, totally lacked all understanding of Alakshyeshvari's spiritual nature; and her mother-in-law, Somp Kunj, had a cruel disposition. Alakshyeshvari's life in this house was difficult and joyless. Her mother-in-law was always finding fault with her. Once she accused Alakshyeshvari of going out at midnight, and made Hiranand suspicious of his wife's fidelity. The truth was that at midnight Alakshyeshvari would go to perform her sadhana (spiritual practice) at the shrine of Mother Sharika on Hara Parvat., Somp Kunj stubbornly refused to change her ways towards Alakshyeshvari. Hiranand also remained foolish and ignorant. Finally, when living there became unbearable, Alakshyeshvari left her husband's house never to return. It is said that this Sapru family's fortunes rapidly declined thereafter. Alakshyeshvari renounced her father's home as well, and decided to seek the eternal abode of the Supreme Being. She wanted to become absorbed in sadhana. Seeking a solitary retreat, she selected a location to the north-east of Srinagar, known by its ancient name Jyestha Rudra. Here she did intense tapasya (austerities) for twelve and a half years, and began to glow with the fire of spirituality. At this point, people, attracted by her spiritual radiance, began to come to her in such large numbers that she decided to leave the place for a more solitary retreat. She moved to a village Mani Gaon, in north Kashmir, on the banks of the Ganges in the foothills of the Himalayas. On festival days many people would gather at Mani Gaon for a dip in the sacred waters. In these beautiful surroundings Alakshyeshvari chose to do her sadhana. On a forested hill-top, far from the village, she made a hermitage for herself. For a long time she remained in solitude, deep in spiritual practices.

Bhawani lived for many years on the banks of the Shahkol, absorbed in meditation. Finally, when large numbers of devotees again began to flock around her, she once more moved away to a quieter spot, in the village of Vaskora. Legend says that the Naga, (snake) Vasuki, did his tapasya in Vaskora to attain the Grace of Shiva. Bhawani had a brother, Lal Jo, who was very devoted to her and took her as his guru. Lal's son, BAL began to stay with her in her service. Once, Lal requested Bhawani to educate his illiterate son. Bhawani gave the boy a pen and ordered him to write. There upon, miraculously, the boy began to write fluently like a highly educated person. The devotees were overwhelmed by this transformation. In Vaskora, Bhawani began to give spiritual instruction to Bal Jo Dar and Sadanand Muttoo in the form of poetical verses, called Vakhs. After twelve and a half years (periods of this length seem to recur in Bhavani's life) had elapsed in Vaskora, Bhawani returned to Srinagar on the entreaties of her numerous devotees, and began to live in Saphakadal.

Many years had elapsed, and Bhawani now yearned to be released from her earthly body. On the Saptami Tithi, in the month of Magha, in the year 1721, Bhavani's soul took flight forever. .

CHAPTER THIRTY-FOUR

PANDIT BIRBAL DHAR

Pandit Birbal Dhar

Kashmiri Hindus did not lose courage despite being victim of atrocities during 500 year barbaric rule of the foreigners. The trend of religious conversion which was started from the reign of Shahmir continued without any interruption for 500 years till the rule of the last Afghan ruler Azim Khan. The erstwhile Hindu Kashmir was converted to a Muslim state on the strength of the sword. During this era all cruel and destructive means were adopted for destroying the Hindu society but despite these cruel and inhuman measures foreign rulers could not finish the basic society of Kashmir. Kashmiri Pundits, while maintaining their tradition of unique sacrifices, protected the Indian value of life. The basic nationalist society of Kashmir had become tired while tolerating and facing atrocities up to the last Afghan Subedar's rule. But their mind for struggle was not tired. The major section of the Pandits was still capable of facing this situation with novel style and this section achieved success through their great sacrifice. The last Subedar, Azim Khan, felt the need of involving capable Pundits for running the administration systematically after silencing the flames of anarchy and mutual conflict. It is condemnable but a reality that every Muslim ruler in Kashmir fully banked on the caliber and wisdom of Pundits for running the state administration and for fulfilling their political objectives and then destroyed the Pandits, their families and their religion for their political interests.

This Subedar, Azim Khan, too obediently followed the demonic traditions of his ancestors and entrusted all the powers of the government to Pt. Birbal Dhar, Pt. Sukh Ram and Mirza Pandit. These three Hindu Sardars were competent administrators. Three distinguished Pandits, namely Sukhram Safaya, Mirza Pandit and Birbal Dhar had been appointed by Afghan governor, Azim Khan, as revenue collectors. Due to crop failure, Birbal Dhar could not collect the expected revenue. The governor insisted that Birbal would have to pay one lac rupees (100,000) to make good the loss. In the coming few days, Birbal, along with many other Pandits, was threatened. Expecting brutal reprisal in keeping with Afghan track record, particularly in the existing intolerable conditions, some distinguished Pandits resolved to turn to the rising power of Sikh empire, headed by Maharaja Ranjit Singh, to save Kashmir from further disaster. Accordingly, Birbal Dhar and his minor son, Raja Kak Dhar left for Lahore in disguise, with a petition signed by prominent Pandits, inviting him to take over the Valley. However, the Afghan governor got wind of it. He unleashed a reign of terror and had many distinguished Pandits killed, their properties confiscated and jaziya imposed on them. He sent his forces to look for Birbal Dhar but to no avail. He, therefore, turned his attention to the latter's wife and his daughter-in-law, who had taken shelter in the house of a trustworthy Muslim, Qadus Gojwari, on the advice of another distinguished and trustworthy Kashmiri Pandit, Vasakak Harkarabashi. The governor tasked Vasakak to look for the two unfortunate women. However, even though Vasakak knew their location, he did not disclose it. All stratagems were tried to make him spill the beans, but he did not budge. A fine of rupees 1000 per day was imposed on him. Yet he maintained his silence. He was subjected to inhuman torture and untold atrocities, but it did not break his resolve. Finally, his abdomen was ripped open and he was brutally murdered. Despite this sacrifice, Azim Khan succeeded in digging out the information about the secret hiding place of these unfortunate women from

Birbal Dhar's son-in-law, Tilak Chand Munshi, who had learnt about the whereabouts of his mother-in-law and his sister in law from his wife. The older woman committed suicide by swallowing a piece of diamond and the younger one was violently converted to Islam and handed over to an Afghan noble who took her to Kabul

Pt. Birbal staked his life

Prominent Pandits of Kashmir decided to protect the Hindu society in this situation. A secret meeting was organized for carrying out the sacred duty of protecting their society in the interest of nationalism. Political, religious and social Hindu leaders from the entire state participated in the meeting which was held in the house of Mirza Pandit. Some decisions were taken after day-long deliberations. The question pertained not only to Kashmir but to whole of India. The question related not only to the Pandit society of Kashmir but to the misfortune having befallen the entire Hindu society. There was need for resolving this misfortune on the national instead of the regional level. After the deliberation it was decided to approach Maharaja Ranjit Singh for help. The responsibility of meeting the Maharaja was given to the seasoned person like Birbal Dhar.

Support of patriotic Muslims

Those patriotic Maliks who helped Birbal and his son in going out of the state were hunted and killed. Those houses, in which Birbal and his son had stayed, were set ablaze and the family members in those houses were burnt to death alive. Their lands were seized and all Government grant and facilities were stopped in all those villages where Birbal and his son had crossed and stayed. The Subedar called Mirza Pandit for talks and the two discussed the situation. During this discussion Mirza Pandit concealed the plan of Birbal. He told the Subedar that if Birbal was successful in reaching the court of Maharaja Ranjit Singh, he would return to Kashmir with Hindu troops or otherwise go to Haridwar for penance. It inflamed the Subedar. He was confident that Birbal would be successful in his mission. He was aware of the patriotism of Maharaja Ranjit Singh and his faith on Hindutva and his powerful country. The Subedar turned mad with anger and through his dexterity Mirza Pandit weakened all the defense of the Subedar. The Subedar started visualizing the fall of the Muslim rule in Kashmir. Subedar Azim Khan started grumbling like an insane animal and whosoever confronted him was killed. When he got wary of all this he ordered that all the women of the family of Birbal Pandit be arrested and brought in front of him. But in this field also he had to face defeat.

Patriotism of Qadis Khan and Pandit Bassa Ram

Prior to his departure, Birbal Pandit had entrusted the task of protection of his family to one of his trusted Muslim associates, Qadis Khan Gojwari. Therefore, both the mother-in-law and her daughter-in-law went to the house of Qadis Khan. The soldiers of Azim Khan launched a massive hunt for the two women but Qadis Khan had made elaborate arrangements for their security and the two women were made part of the family in order to prevent any suspicion from taking shape.

One Hindu, Pandit Bassa Ram, knew about the whereabouts of the two women. He had left the two women in the house of Qadis Khan. Bassa Ram was a close friend of Birbal Pandit. Subedar Azim Khan learnt about the whereabouts of Bassa Ram who was arrested and brought to the subedar. The Subedar gave him the allurements of estates, gold and top post in the Government but the strong-willed Pandit refused to divulge anything. The Subedar ordered that the Pandit should be tortured for nine days he was kept hungry and was subjected to torture. His flesh was peeled off with hot iron rods. His eyes were gouged out and for each of these nine days he was fined Rs. 9,000. But when he refused to open his mouth despite undergoing all these ordeals and tortures, on the 10th day his belly was ripped open with red hot sword and this way Bassa Ram Kak achieved martyrdom on the altar of the nation.

Victory campaign of Sikh soldiers

Maharaja Ranjit Singh sent his five top and brave Army commanders along with 30,000 soldiers to Kashmir under the guidance of Pandit Birbal. Raja Gulab Singh of Jammu, and other powerful Army officers including Hari Singh Nalwa, Jwala Singh, Hukum Singh and Shyam Singh uprooted the troops of Jabbar Khan with their might. Jabbar Khan took to his heels. The Sikh soldiers emerged victorious and this way brought about an end of the Afghan rule. On June 20, 1819 A.D. Pandit Birbal entered with Sikh soldiers into Kashmir as a victor. The Sikhs were highly shocked at the sight of havoc that had been wrought on the Kashmiri Pandits all through the period the Muslims held sway over Kashmir. Their temples had been ravaged and leveled; they were butchered and murdered; they were not permitted to worship their gods and goddesses and their women-folk were abducted for export to Kabul. They were burdened with unjust and iniquitous Twenty eight Afghan governors ruled Kashmir during the 67 years of their despotic occupation. It can safely be said that the corner-stone of Afghan rule in Kashmir was terror and the only legacy they left behind was their resort to brutality and savage torture.

Finally, came the turn of Vasakak Harkarabashi. His abdomen was ripped open and his dead body trampled upon. To quench his thirst for retribution, Azim Khan continued with the terror that he had let loose on the innocent and peaceful Pandits. In his paranoia he rounded up all those whom he suspected of being in league with Birbal Dhar. He sent them all to a concentration camp established near Nishat garden, where numerous atrocities were committed on them. The kind of torture inflicted on them knew no bounds. Azim Khan left Kashmir in 1816 with 20 million rupees, leaving the Valley in the care of his younger brother, Jabbar Khan, who perhaps, was the cruelest of all Afghan governors.

As if this was not enough, between 1812 and 1816, many unsuccessful attempts were made by Shahmir's and Chaks to annex Kashmir. This resulted in continued strife which tore the fabric of Kashmiri society and left deep scars on it.

Birbal Dhar, in the meanwhile, succeeded in convincing Maharaja Ranjit Singh to annex Kashmir and bring to an end the cruel rule of the Afghans. He promised to compensate the Maharaja if the Sikhs were unable to take Kashmir. As a guarantee, he left behind his son Raja Kak Dhar with the king. However, the guarantee remained un-cashed as the Sikh forces finally entered the valley under Mirsa Dewan Chand on July 15, 1819, and annexed the Valley. Jabbar Khan's defeat brought to an end the inglorious rule of Afghans.

The magnanimity of Kashmiri Pandits and their regard for religious tolerance can be gauged from some incidents that took place immediately after the Sikhs annexed the Valley. In those troubled times there appeared no guarantee for the safe treatment of Afghan women, particularly when seen in the background of the treatment meted out to Pandit women in general and to the wife and daughter of Birbal Dhar in particular. However, Afghan womenfolk were saved only because of the intervention of an illustrious Pandit, Sahajram. On his advice they were sent to Kabul, escorted by Sahajram himself. That was how a Kashmiri Pandit saved the honor of Afghan women, when their own women had been treated so shabbily.

Another incident concerns the impending demolition of the mosque of Shah Hamadan. Some Sikhs were determined to knock down this mosque. When Muslims learnt of it, they sent a delegation under Syed Hassan Shah Khanyari to Birbal Dhar to plead with him to use his influence with the Sikhs to dissuade them from going ahead with the destruction of this mosque. Birbal Dhar moved swiftly in the matter and convinced the Sikhs that it was not the right thing to do and thus saved it from being destroyed. Historian, GMD Sufi, acknowledges it to the lasting credit of the true character and nobility of the distinguished Kashmiri Pandit. Subsequently, Diwan Moti Ram was appointed by the Sikhs as their first governor, with Birbal Dhar as his Peshkar (Chief Local Advisor).

CHAPTER THIRTY-FIVE

ARNIMAL

Arnimal

E

ighteenth century Kashmiri romantic poet was a path-breaker in her own right. Born in a conservative Kashmiri Hindu society, she lived in a loveless marriage, forsaken by her husband. She married Munshi Bhawani Das Kachroo, a poet from Rainawari and an erudite Persian scholar in the court of Jumma Khan, the Afghan Governor of Kashmir between 1788 and 1792.Her husband Bhawani Das Kachroo was a more accomplished poet. But poetry is not only about accomplishments. He, however, was not interested in her. He was known to abandon her and philander in the world In Arni's case poetry rose from the heart, got welled up in the breast and out came the pathetic gems of Kashmiri literature. For her, speaking of her marital woes was an act of grave defiance. Much like her stylistic predecessor Habba Khatoon, Arnimal's poetry had an earthy quality, a relevance and place in her time, drawing from reality without the mystical allusions other Kashmiri poets are often known for. Her words, however, do take us back to Habba's floral poems. Not wanting to be silent and cast off, she sang of her woes and exposed her husband's infidelity. She was a woman spurned, and her poetry told tales of her dejection. For Arnimal to speak of violence and abuse while embedded in a culture of silence was an admirable and courageous feat. Her words of broken heartedness ring loud, reminding us of the suffering women often endure behind closed doors. Arnimal was born in Palhalan during the eighteenth century. In all types of poetry, feelings get converted to thought and thought by conversion to word. In Arni's case spoken word with feeling produced still effect and impact is heard more than two centuries after her death. In 18th Century Kashmir amidst the tyranny of Afghans and in the midst of bountiful Kashmir nature, life was hard and painful in her parents' home. She sought solace in nature or mixed nature to create poetic effect. Arnimal does not give us philosophical teaching or inspired and complex religions sermons as in the case of Lal Ded. She highlights her condition with simplicity and charm. Her state is sad but creates powerful emotion to hide that sadness or creates poetry for solace. Arnimal and Habba Khatoon seem to have similar sort of image and feeling. They mirror each other in every respect. Both or they do not impose their poetry. Lal Ded is special because of power, punch she generates in her Vakhs. Arnimal and Habba Khatoon is product of nature. They seldom rise above it as in the case of Lal Ded. In fact both Arnimal and Habba Khatoon are overwhelmed by nature. But rise at appropriate time in order not to drown.

CHAPTER THIRTY-SIX

THE DOGRA RULE IN KASHMIR

The Dogra rule (November 1846 to October 1947)

The Dogra rule which lasted for exactly one hundred and one years from November 1846 to October 1947, was one of the most peaceful and progressive periods in the long history of the Kashmir valley and other constituent parts of the Jammu and Kashmir State. The credit for opening much of this far flung mountainous territory of snow covered peaks, deep ravines, extensive valleys and arid Himalayan plateaus to modern civilization and social and political influence, of which the present Kashmir problem is a direct result, goes to its Dogra rulers. The Kashmir valley which is the most celebrated and coveted part of the State is particularly indebted to them. They lavished their attention and resources on it even at the cost of their homeland - Jammu, in order to make it an attractive tourist resort. The first task of Gulab Singh after having obtained possession of Kashmir and its surrounding territories was to consolidate them and give them an effective and efficient administration. From the point of view of consolidation, Gilgit was the only area over which his grip was still not very firm. There took place a serious uprising in Gilgit in 1851 with the help of the Rajas of Yasin, Hunza and Nagar as a result of which the entire Dogra garrison there was cut to pieces. Only a Gurkha woman swam across the Indus to tell the story of this disaster. It was a great blow to the prestige of Gulab Singh who was then in failing health. For the time being he had to accept the Indus as frontier between his kingdom and Gilgit proper. Even though he could not recapture Gilgit in his lifetime, he laid the foundations of a sound and stable administration in the rest of his territories which enabled his son, Ranbir Singh, to reconquer Gilgit and its adjoining areas. He divided the State into two provinces, each under a Governor, and two frontier areas each under a 'Thanedar'.Jammu Province covered the entire territory from the Ravi to the Jhelum lying south of the Pir Panchal range. It included the whole of Dugar region together with Mirpur area of the western Punjabi speaking belt. Kashmir province included the whole of Kashmir valley and the western district of Muzfarabad. The valley was divided into two districts Anantnag which included the city of Srinagar and the strategic roads linking the valley with Jammu and Laddakh and Baramulla which covered north-western parts of the valley adjoining Muzfarabad and Poonch. Srinagar was made the summer capital of the State; which until then was governed from Jammu. The frontier region of Laddakh was put under the charge of a Thanedar. A number of efficient and capable Thanedar like Magna, Mehta Basti Ram and Mehta Mangal gave modern administration to Laddakh for the first time. They built the fort and bazaar of Leh, laid plantations for a perennial supply of fuel, built and repaired bridle roads linking Leh with Srinagar, Lahaul, Yarkand and Gartok, surveyed the traditional Laddakh-Tibet frontier and made a land settlement for the first time. Baltistan with its main town of Skardu was put under the charge of another Thanedar. Later, both Laddakh and Baltistan were joined together and put under the charge of one administrator who had his headquarters at Leh in summer and Skardu in winter. Gilgit area when reconquered in 1860 was made a separate administrative unit with its headquarters in the town of Gilgit. This administrative set up continued right until the end of Dogra rule in 1947.As a compromise settlement with the Raja of Chamba who claimed Bhadarwah as a part of his possessions; he was allowed to transfer his allegiance to the British instead of the Dogra King in return for renunciation of any claim on Bhadarwah. No wonder that the people of Bhadarwah continue to yearn for reunion with Chamba through unification of Himachal Pradesh and Jammu region. The British, as has been said above, handed over Kashmir to Gulab Singh in 1846 because they had no alternative at that time. But after the annexation of Punjab, a number of British officials began to have second thoughts regarding the Treaty of Amritsar. Pressure began to be put on Gulab Singh to accept a British Resident like other Indian States and give some other concessions to the British. But Gulab Singh took a firm stand on the Treaty of 1846 and refused to yield in the matter. The British though frustrated in their attempt continued to look for an opportunity to bring down Jammu and Kashmir to the level of other Indian States. Maharaja Gulab Singh died in 1858 and was succeeded by Ranbir Singh whom he had installed on the throne with his own hands in 1856. He had himself functioned as Governor of Kashmir province during the last two years of his life.

Ranbir Singh

The most outstanding achievement of Ranbir Singh, who is considered to be the greatest of the Dogra rulers, was the reconquest of Gilgit and subjugation of the frontier states of Hunza and Nagar. He organized a big expedition to which almost every Dogra family contributed a soldier in 1860 under the command of Colonel Devi Singh. It inflicted a crushing defeat on the Rajas and thus avenged the earlier Dogra defeat. Chitral also accepted his sovereignty in 1876.After having thus re-established the prestige of the Dogra army; he turned his attention to internal reforms. The Ranbir 'Dand-Vidhi', the code of laws, both civil and criminal, which he got prepared, established his reputation as a law-giver. He reorganized his army on the European model but with Sanskrit terms of Command. His spirit of independence and the originality and initiative he displayed in the organization of his civil and military administration were not to the liking of the British. They, therefore, made another attempt to force a British Resident on Jammu and Kashmir in 1873. But like Gulab Singh, Ranbir Singh too refused to yield in the matter on the plea that there was no provision in the Treaty of 1846 giving authority to the British Government to appoint a Resident. The British felt very much chagrined and took resort to other methods for achieving their objective. Taking advantage of mutual bickering between Pratap Singh, the eldest son of Ranbir Singh, and his two younger brothers, Ram Singh and Amar Singh, they made acceptance of a British Resident a pre-condition for giving recognition to his successor after his death in 1885.A major event of Maharaja Ranbir Singh's reign which could have changed the whole course of history of Kashmir was the collective approach of Kashmir Muslims to him for being taken back into the Hindu fold.

Pratap Singh

Having got a Resident appointed which eventually brought down Jammu and Kashmir to the level of other Indian States like Hyderabad and Gwalior, the British now made a determined bid to have a more direct control over the State The Maharaja was charged with conspiring with Russia against the British and was forced to hand over all his powers to a five members State Council which ran the administration under the guidance of the British Resident for many years. In the meantime, the British interest in the Pamirs and the frontier states of Chitral, Hunza was aroused by the continued advance of Czarist Russia in Central Asia. As a result, the British decided to have a more effective control over the Mehtar of Chitral. The military campaign launched for the purpose between 1889 and 1895 was eonducted by the State forces but under the command of British officers. After the successful termination of the campaign, Chitral passed under direct control of the British in practice. But in theory it continued to be a feudatory of Maharaja of Jammu and Kashmir.

This campaign brought the strategic importance of Gilgit region to the notice of the British. The publication of White's book "WHERE THREE EMPIRES MEET" which gave a graphic account of this campaign and the valor of Dogra troops put Gilgit on the map of the world. The result was a concerted effort on the part of the British Government to bring the whole of Gilgit area under its direct control. For the moment a British political agent was stationed at Gilgit to watch British interests though administrative control remained in the hands of the State Government. Maharaja Pratap Singh got back full powers in 1905 after an attempt to completely oust him had been foiled by the timely revelation of the machinations of the Political Department of the British Government of India in the "AMRIT BAZAR PATRIKA" of Calcutta and raising of the issue in the British House of Commons by some opposition members. He ruled for twenty years more till his death in 1925.The modernization of Jammu and Kashmir State began during the reign of Pratap Singh. Kashmir was linked to Rawalpindi,

Abbotabad and Sialkot by motor able roads, first rate Arts and Science Colleges were opened in Jammu and Srinagar, foreign administration was streamlined with the help of British experts, a hydro- electric plant, among the first few of its kind in India, was set up at Mehura near Baramulla and new holiday resorts like Gulmarg and Pahalgam were developed in the Valley.

Hari Singh

This process of modernization of the State was accelerated by the succession to the throne of his young, intelligent but impulsive nephew, Maharaja Hari Singh in 1925. He had spent many years of his early life in England which had created in him a strong urge to develop and modernize his State, particularly the Kashmir Valley. This urge was partly the result of a new awareness in his mind about the importance of his State and a distrust of the British whose bullying attitude had created a strong reaction in his young and self-conscious mind. His misunderstanding with the British Resident began from the very day of his coronation and continued to grow in the succeeding years due to his spirit of independence. The breaking point however was brought by his speech at the first Round Table Conference in London in 1930 in the course of which he said: "While Indian Princes valued British connection, they had full sympathy for the aspirations of their motherland for an equal and honorable place in the comity of nations." This outspoken support to the "Seditious" demand for independence by the foremost representative of Princely India, which had been given a disproportionately high representation at the Round Table Conference to counterbalance the popular representatives from British India, came as a bomb shell to the British diehards in England and the Political Department in India. The strategic importance of Jammu and Kashmir State and the British plan to have a more direct control over Gilgit made this spirit of independence and defiance in Hari Singh all the more galling to them, so they decided to break him. To that end they had recourse to the convenient method of building up popular "Muslim" pressure on communal basis. This led to the beginning of a socio-religious movement in the State which provided the religion- political background of the events which culminated in the emergence of the Kashmir problem in its present form. The British aim was achieved. The Gilgit region was ceded to the British by the Maharaja on a sixty year lease in 1935. This brought the whole of Gilgit including the frontier States of Hunza and Nagar directly under the control of the British Political Agent stationed at Gilgit. These political developments did not deter Hari Singh from pursuing his plans for the modernization of Kashmir valley in which he took a special pride. Apart from the meager resources of the State, he spent huge sums from his accumulated family treasures as well as his own privy purse to beautify the valley and equip it with modern amenities for Indian and foreign tourists. It would be no exaggeration to say that the modern embellishments which have made Kashmir valley such a rage with foreign tourists are mainly his contribution to this 'Paradise' on earth. Had he bestowed even a fraction of the interest and money he lavished on Kashmir valley on his own homeland of Jammu which also abounds in places of great natural beauty and is the richest part of the State from the point of view of human, forest and mineral resources Hari Singh had to leave the state in 1949 under pressure of the Government of India which was being blackmailed by Sheikh Abdullah. His son, Crown Prince Karan Singh was made constitutional head of the state "Sadar - I - Riyasat" under the new constitution of Jammu And Kashmir State. Hari Singh never looked back. He died in Bombay in 1961.

CHAPTER THIRTY-SEVEN

GENERAL ZORAWAR SINGH

General Zorawar Singh

General Zorawar Singh Kahluria (1784–12 December 1841) was a military general of ruler Gulab Singh of Jammu, who was a vassal of the Sikh Empire He served as the governor (Wazir-e-Wazarat) of Kisthwar and extended the territories of the kingdom by conquering Laddakh and Baltistan. He also boldly attempted the conquest of West Tibet but was killed in battle of during the Sikh-Tibetan war. In reference to his legacy of conquests in the Himalaya Mountains including Laddakh, Tibet, Baltistan and Skardu as General and Wazir, Zorawar Singh has been referred to as the Napoleon of India

Early life and career

He was born in September 1784 in a Hindu Kahluria Rajput family in the princely state of Kahlur (Bilaspur) state, in present day Himachal Pradesh.

Very little is known about his early life. He left his home at an early age of 16 and took up a job as a private servant of Rana Jaswant Singh, Jagirdar of present day Ramnagar. It was here that he learnt riding, archery and swordsmanship. Afterwards he joined as a sepoy of Kiladar of Reasi. Being brave, intelligent and enterprising he won favors of his master. Kiladar assigned him the duties of carrying messages to Raja Gulab Singh at Jammu. It was during one of these meetings with Raja Gulab Singh when he brought into his notice certain flaws and wastages that were occurring in Raja's supply department. He even gave an alternative plan of supplies. When implemented, the new plan affected lots of savings. Impressed, Gulab Singh promoted him as inspector of the commissariat of supplies for all the forts North of Jammu. After the occupation of Kisthwar in 1821, he was made its Hakim (Governor). Later when Gulab Singh became ruler of Jammu in 1822, he elevated Zorawar Singh to the status of Governor of Reasi, Arnas and Kussal and awarded him the title of Wazir. Zorawar Singh fulfilled his task and his grateful ruler made him commissariat officer of all forts north of Jammu. He was later made governor of Kisthwar and was given the title of Wazir (minister).

Even though it was a newly conquered region Zorawar had no trouble in keeping the peace; many of the local Rajput were recruited into his army. In 1835 the nearby region of Paddar was taken from Chamba (now in Himachal Pradesh) in the course of a battle. Paddar later became known for its sapphire mines. But this was a mere sideshow to General Zorawar Singh's more famous expeditions, on which he had already embarked in the previous year.

The Ladhak campaigns

To the east of Kisthwar and Kashmir are the snow-clad mountains of the upper Himalayas the rivers of Zanskar Gorge, Suru River, and Drass rise from these snows, and flow across the plateau of Ladhak into the Indus River. Several petty principalities in this region were tributary to the Gyalpo of Ladhak (King). In 1834 one of these, the Raja of Timbus, sought Zorawars help against the Gyalpo. Meanwhile, the Rajput general had been burning to distinguish himself by expanding the territory of Raja Gulab Singh also at that time, according to the Gulab Nama, Kisthwar went through a drought that caused a loss of revenue and forced Zorawar to extract money through war.

The Rajputs of Jammu and Himachal have traditionally excelled in mountain fighting; therefore Zorawar had no trouble in crossing the mountain ranges and entering Ladhak through the source of the Suru River where his 5000 men defeated an army of local Botis.After moving to Kargil and subduing the landlords along the way Zorawar received the submission of the Ladhaki however Tsepal Namgyal, the Gyalpo (ruler), sent his general Banko Kahlon by a roundabout route to cut off Zorawars communications. The astute general doubled back to Kartse, where he sheltered his troops through the winter. In the spring of 1835 he defeated the large Ladhaki army of Banko Kahlon and marched his victorious troops towards Leh. The Gyalpo now agreed to pay 50,000 rupees as war-indemnity and 20,000 rupees as an annual tribute.

Alarmed at the gains of the Dogras, the governor of Kashmir, Mehan Singh, incited the Ladhaki chieftains to rebel but Zorawar quickly marched back to the Himalayan valleys and subdued the rebels, now forcing the Raja of Zanskar to also pay a separate tribute to Jammu. But in 1836 Mehan Singh, who was in correspondence with the Lahore durbar, this time instigated the Gyalpo to revolt Zorawar force-marched his army in ten days to surprise the Ladhaki and forced them to submit. He now built a fort outside Leh and placed there a garrison of 300 men under Dalel Singh the Gyalpo was deposed to an estate and a Ladhaki general, Ngorub Stanzin, was made King. But the latter did not prove to be loyal hence the Gyalpo was restored to his throne in 1838.

Baltistan campaign

To the northwest of Ladhak, and to the north of Kashmir, lies the region of Baltistan. Muhammad Shah, the son of the ruler of Skardu, Raja Ahmad Shah, fled to Leh and sought the aid of the Gyalpo and Zorawar against his father. But some of the Ladhaki nobles allowed Ahmad Shah to imprison his son and sought his aid in a general rebellion against the Dogras. After defeating the Ladhaki rebels Zorawar invaded Baltistan in the winter of 1839/40, adding a large contingent of Ladhaki to his army. The advance brigade of 5,000 under Nidhan Singh lost its way in the cold and snow and was surrounded by the enemy; many soldiers perished from the cold. Then Mehta Basti Ram, a prominent Rajput from Kisthwar, established contact with the main force. On their arrival the Botis of Skardu were defeated and forced to flee. They were chased to the fort of Skardu which was invested by Zorawar for a few days. One night the Dogras scaled the steep mountain behind the fort and after some fighting captured the small fort on its crest. From this position the next day they began firing down at the main fort and forced the Raja to surrender. Zorawar built a fort on the banks of the Indus where he placed a contingent of his soldiers.

After placing Muhammad Shah on the throne for an annual tribute of 7000 rupees, a Dogra contingent under Wazir Lakhpat advanced westwards, conquered the fort of Astor and took its Darad Raja prisoner. However this Raja was tributary to Mehan Singh, the governor of Kashmir, who was alarmed at the Dogra conquests since they only expanded the kingdom of Gulab Singh while not bringing any benefit to the Lahore durbar. His complaint at Lahore was forwarded to Raja Gulab Singh at Jammu and he ordered the Darad Raja to be released.

Tibet expedition

One column under the Ladhaki prince, Nono Sungnam, followed the course of the Indus River to its source. Another column of 300 men, under Ghulam Khan, marched along the mountains leading up to the Kailas Range and thus south of the Indus. Zorawar himself led 3,000 men along the plateau region where the vast and picturesque Panging Lake is located. Sweeping all resistance before them, the three columns passed the Lake Manasarovar and converged at Gartok, defeating the small Tibetan force stationed there. The enemy commander fled to Taklakot but Zorawar stormed that fort on 6 September 1841. Envoys from Tibet now came to him as did agents of the Maharaja of Nepal, whose kingdom was only fifteen miles from Taklakot.

On my arrival at Taklakot a force of only about 1,000 local troops could be mustered, which was divided and stationed as guards at different posts. A guard post was quickly established at a strategic pass near Taklakot to stop the invaders, but these local troops were not brave enough to fight off the Dogras and fled at the approach of the invaders .Zorawar and his men now went on pilgrimage to Manasarovar and Mount Kailash. He had extended his communication and supply line over 450 miles of inhospitable terrain by building small forts and pickets along the way. The fort Chi-Tang was built near Taklakot, where Mehta Basti Ram was put in command of 500 men, with 8 or 9 cannon. With the onset of winter all the passes were blocked and roads snowed in. The supplies for the Dogra army over such a long distance failed despite Zorawars meticulous preparations. As the intense cold, coupled with the rain, snow and lightning continued for weeks upon weeks, many of the soldiers lost their fingers and toes to frostbite. Others starved to death, while some burnt the wooden stock of their muskets to warm themselves. The Tibetans and their Chinese allies regrouped and advanced to give battle, bypassing the Dogra fort of Chi-Tang. Zorawar and his men met them at the Battle of To-yo on 12 December 184 in the early exchange of fire the Rajput general was wounded .This final campaign against Tibet which turned out to be fatal for him and disastrous for the Dogra expansion plan.

CHAPTER THIRTY-EIGHT

MADHAV KOUL (UNSUNG HERO OF 1931)

Madhav Koul (Unsung Hero of 1931)

Late Madhav koul savior of Hindus of shopian was martyred by Muslim religious fanatic on the Kila Bagh in 1931 .He was a court official (Nazir) in shopian court and was on duty. He was brutally killed while saving small children trapped in a school, his eyes were taken out with sharp edges knives and his body was mutilated.

During 1931 there was religious uprising which were initiated by the people from outside Kashmir. The communal riots that engulfed Srinagar

(Kashmir) on July 13, 1931 were the culmination of prolonged intrigues by the British to violate the Treaty of Amritsar, signed with Maharaja Gulab Singh in 1846, founder of the kingdom of Jammu and Kashmir. Their aim was to control the Northern Frontiers of India to keep an eye on the ethnic tribes that inhabited these regions, and Russian advances. They were aware that the Himalayas, of which the State of Jammu and Kashmir was a critical constituent, defined the civilization and cultural moorings of the Indian Nation. July 13 is an important date in Kashmir. In 1931, on this day in Srinagar and later on for months elsewhere too, the first ever organized communal carnage in the recorded history of modern Kashmir took place. Hundreds were murdered, burnt alive, and tossed into the river, molested, raped, robbed and even forcibly converted to Islam. When the rioters were challenged and sought to be controlled by the police, a few of them died. The dead rioters were hailed as martyrs by their cohorts. It was only later, in independent India no less, that the state government of Jammu and Kashmir formally sanctified those criminals and decided to commemorate the dead rioters as fallen heroes, every year on July 13. Politics apart it is important to know the facts of what happened then. In 1931, Maharaja Hari Singh was the sovereign ruler of the Jammu and Kashmir, which included Laddakh, Gilgit-Baltistan, Muzfarabad-Mirpur, Aksai Chin and Saksham Valley. The British wanted him to lease them the Gilgit agency. The Maharaja was reluctant. He was a rare Hindu king who ruled over his predominantly Muslim subjects. They decided to turn a few screws. An Ahmadi (now declared non Muslims of government of Pakistan) from Peshawar Abdul Qadir was brought into Srinagar by the British intelligence in the garb of a cook for the local British resident .A public meeting was organized at the Shah-e-Hamadan, Khanqah Mohalla. There, Abdul Qadir delivered a fiery speech. He quoted liberally from the Quran to incite the Muslims against the Maharaja. Spewing communal venom and inflaming passion, he asserted that the book forbade Muslims to subject themselves to an infidel Hindu ruler. He also incited them to cow slaughter, which was forbidden under the law. Qadir was ordered to be arrested for sedition. His arrest was resisted. Later his trial too was sought to be disrupted repeatedly. It was then decided to hold his trial in the jail premises itself. The hearing in jail fell on 13th July. On that day, a mob stormed the jail and demanded admittance along with the Sessions Judge. When the Judge had passed the gates, the crowd also attempted to get in. The other gates had been forced and the inner gates were attacked. At the suggestion of the Judge, two

Muslim lawyers, representing the accused, harangued the visitors to go out of the Jail precincts. Finding that there was no possibility of ingress, the crowd went out and started stoning officials and set fire to the police lines. The police force was then called in. All efforts to pacify the unruly mob proved futile. While there was commotion outside the jail there was also disturbance inside, prisoners tried to force open the iron gates. About this time, certain prisoners were being taken from the court to the jail. The crowd stoned the policemen and the prisoners were liberated. The prospect was by no means satisfactory. The District Magistrate's order was defied, who had been summoned to the spot by the time, and had declared the crowd to be an "unlawful assembly" and ordered its dispersal. The order was defied and finding that the mob could neither be pacified nor dispersed, the District Magistrate directed fire to be opened. The crowd fell off but later it re-assembled and resumed stoning. It had to be dispersed with a Lathi charge. Part of the crowd, however moved towards the Hari Parbat Fort: the cavalry had to pursue it and disperse it again. A section of the recalcitrant's proceeded towards a place called Maharaj Ganj which is a business locality and loot over an extensive area followed. From Bhori Kadal to Alikadal a long stretch, Hindu shops were raided. Other localities such as Safakadal and Nawakadal too formed the centers of loot. Bazaar streets were littered with property, books of accounts were burnt: the Hindu shopkeepers were molested, in short, pandemonium prevailed. The Hindu merchants lost lakhs worth of goods. The most extraordinary portion of the story was that almost simultaneously with the happenings at Srinagar, there was an uprising at a place named Vicharnag, some 5 or 6 miles away. It has been stated that untold atrocities were committed there; men owning lakhs were reduced to indigence and women were subjected to the worst possible and the most indecent assaults. A military force was dispatched to the place, but by that time the havoc had been completed. Elsewhere too, the Hindus were the victims of ambuscade. Some lost their lives and many suffered physical injuries. Stray assaults continued till long after. It was an Islamist rebellion against the Hindu king. Sheikh Abdullah too was found complicit in the uprising. He was arrested, tried, convicted and sent to prison. But soon in 1932, he was pardoned by the Maharaja and released within a few months without completing the sentence. But aftershocks continued over into weeks and months. It also wrecked havoc in far flung Rajouri, Kotli and Mirpur. Innocents were mercilessly killed and many were converted to Islam forcibly. Religious places of worship, of Hindus and Sikhs, that is. Temples and Gurudwaras, all met with the same fate. Many were completely damaged and desecrated. In other few cases, though buildings were not damaged, yet the sacred idols and holy books, including the Guru Granth Sahib, were badly damaged burnt and desecrated. These happenings known as "88 NA SHAURASH" (Riots of 1988 Bikram or 1931 Christian Era) are still in the memory of not only the survivors of that time but also of their subsequent generations, and the refugees of 1947, scattered throughout India and awaiting Rehabilitation. To calm down the situation Maharaja Hari Singh organized the visit of Maulana Abdul Kalam Azad and Tej Bahadur Sapru. They tried to dissuade Muslims leaders of Kashmir about their struggle, campaigned in valley and asked people to cooperate with the Maharaja's government. This resulted in pacifying some Muslim leaders for some time. And through the intervention of a liberal Muslim politician from British India Meher shah, an agreement was achieved between Muslim leaders of Kashmir and the government. The agreement is known as Temporary truce. The propaganda against started in Jama Masjid on August 28, 1931 which made public were very angry. Subsequently the revolt began to ripen. The arrests of several Muslim leaders on 21st September 1931, the breaches of Temporary truce and conspiracies like Riots Enquiry Commission, heated Muslim rage into agitation. Complete hartal was observed. 24th day of September 193 Mirwaiz Yusuf Shah gave a new turn to the movement in September 1931. He called for Jihad, much to the annoyance of the Maharaja. Mirwaizs call evoked massive response. Thousands of people came out with shovels, axes, sticks and assembled at Khanyar near Dastgeer Sahib's shrine on September 24. Some people were also armed with guns. However, no untoward incident took place. On same fateful day 24th September 1931 angry mob shouting slogans against the Maharaja had been moving towards the Munsif court and police station. They mob wanted to immediate release a Pir (Molvi) who was facing trail in Munsif court shopian for the seduction charges Sensing the trouble which this religious fanatic mob may create in the town and may target the Hindu minority and their properties. Madhav koul after receiving this information immediately asked the Hindu shopkeeper close the shop and move home mostly belonged to near Hindu village Bhatpara. But most of these people were reluctant to move as their children are trapped in the school. He told them you just move out and he will take care of them, He straight away moved towards the middle school and shifted children to safer place and moved towards the court during the time he was taped by the crowd at

Kila Bagh and was brutally killed and his body was mutilated. After that angry crowd when on the rampage dismantled and became unstoppable one storey of the police station with the stoning and staring burning public and Hindu minority properties. When crowd went out of control police was forced to fire. This was the first time in the history of shopian bullet was fired. In the late evening army came and took control the situation when crowd disbursed. On same day 24th September Maharaja Government issued a ordinance called 19L which gave powers to the army officers and district magistrates to arrest and search without warrant on suspicious people After that Maharaja Government came in to the action search was launched for the killers and main accused Khalil Banday in the neighboring towns and villages culprits Mohammad Sultan Nengroo Abdul Gaffar and Mohammad wani were arrested and main accused Khalil Banday remained absconding. When new government was formed under Sheikh Mohammad Abdullah brutal killers of Madhav koul were declared freedom fighters and their families were given pension by the by the state government after 1948

CHAPTER THIRTY-NINE

PAKISTAN ATTACK KASHMIR (1947)

Pakistan's attack on Kashmir (1947)

In 1947 the Maharaja of Jammu and Kashmir refused to accede to either India or to Pakistan. The Pakistanis in a bid to pressurize the Maharaja to accede to Pakistan first ensured an economic blockade, then small-scale skirmishes at the border and then invaded the state using a combination of tribal's and Pakistani troops code named Operation Gulmarg under Major General Akbar Khan, who styled himself General Jebel Tariq. But at lost moment tribal men refused to obey as they were not given the payment as was decided earlier every tribal volunteers was to be paid rupees 3500 . Major General Akbar Khan told them that payment will be paid only after operation completed. This angered the tribal leaders and they decided to abandon the operation. Till the time national conference leaders Sheikh Abdullah who was released from the prison declared in an executive council meeting of the party held on 5th October 1947 that his party is going to support either independent Kashmir or will support the ascension with India and will not at any cost join the rouge state Pakistan led by Jinnah. When this shocking news reached the Jinnah he held an emergency meeting with the Major General Akbar Khan asked him to sort out the problem of tribal leader. After that had Major General Akbar Khan meeting with tribal and convinced them that their role is only to loot and create law and order problem they need not to fight war with regular army Indian army if they arrive on the scene. But only have to support the Pakistan army when taking on the state forces. They were not still convinced after that he gifted tribal leaders 3 Samovars made up of brass but its handle was made of gold he told that this kind of Samovar is used by Kashmiri Pandits to make tea. Because of these Samovars gifted to them the tribal leaders agreed for the operation. It is believed that these Samovars where gifted to Jinnah by the Dewan of Junagarh Shah Nawaz Bhutto grad father of Benazir Bhutto

According to Operation Gulmarg plan every Pathan tribe was required to enlist at least one Lashkar of 1000 tribesmen. Separate instructions for their recruitment were issued to the Deputy Commissioners and Political Agents. After enlistment these Lashkars were to be concentrated at Bannu, Wana, Peshawar, Kohat, Thal and Nowshera by the first week of September 1947. The Brigade Commanders at these places were to issue them arms, ammunition and some essential items of clothing are, on paper showing these issues against some Pakistan Army units. Each Tribal Lashkar was also to be provided with a Major, a Captain and ten JCOs of the regular Pakistan Army. The Major was to be the actual commander of the Lashkar and act as the adviser of the tribal Malik nominally in command of the unit. The Captain was to act as staff officer, while each of the ten JCOs was to be in charge of a company or group of the Lashkar. These Pakistan regulars were to be Pathans and to dress and live exactly like the other Pathans in the Lashkar. The entire force was to be commanded by Maj-Gen Akbar Khan, who was given the code name Tariq. He was to be assisted by Brigadier Sher Khan. Their HQ was located in the same building as the C-in-C of the Pakistan.

About 7000-8000 raiders aided by regulars (officers and junior commissioned officers) of the Pakistan army advanced towards Srinagar. The tribesmen supported by Pakistani soldiers swarmed across the Jhelum

River and began systematic plunder, arson, rape and mindless killing of the unarmed and innocent people of Jammu and Kashmir. State forces headquarters at Srinagar was informed and Brigadier Rajinder Singh reached Uri on October 23, 1947. The force of approximately one company held out against about 4000 tribesmen till October 24, 1947 and later withdrew to Mohura.Despite high casualties the soldiers were able to hold the enemy till October 26, 1947, when they were overrun and almost all of them perished fighting. Brig Rajinder Singh, killed in the attack, was awarded the Mahavir Chakra posthumously.

The raiders entered Baramulla town on October 26, 1947 and promptly set about raping, plundering and killing. Hindus, Sikhs and Muslims were killed and looted without discrimination while women were forcibly abducted to be sold in the streets of Rawalpindi and Peshawar or to live as slaves in distant tribal territories. Mohammad Maqbol Sherwani was tortured and shot to death in public for rousing the locals to resist the invaders. While Baramulla was being ransacked, Maharaja Hari Singh requested military assistance from the government of India, paving the way for induction of Indian troops in Jammu and Kashmir, he added. The Maharaja later signed an instrument of accession with India, which was accepted by the then Governor General. On November 7, Sherwani was caught, nailed to a post through the palms and chest and brutally cut down by a volley of 14 bullets.

Muzfarabad fell within a few hours of the attack and the invaders proceeded towards Baramulla, Sopore and Srinagar. At the Uri Bridge Brigadier Rajinder Singh lost his life putting up a valiant fight .He held the invaders for two days which gave time to the Maharajah to flee the valley and the Indian Army to intervene. The Pakistani invaders entered Baramulla on October 26, 1947 and proceeded to indulge in Rape, murder, loot and arson, especially targeting Sikhs and Kashmiri Pandit community. By the morning of October 27th some raiders had reached the outskirts of Srinagar. Hari Singh's exit had totally broken the morale of the government and security establishment. Police stations were empty. Anything could happen at any time. Sheikh Abdullah and his National Conference organized a voluntary force of young men known as Salamati Fauj in the city with specific direction to maintain communal harmony at all costs. This worked; Halka Committees became the police station.

Massacre of Hindus and Sikhs in Mirpur

The Mirpur massacre will go down in history as one of the worst genocides of mankind. On November 25, 1947, the historic city of Mirpur fell to the tribal raiders, who were aided and abetted by Pakistan. On that unforgettable day men, women and children embarked on their uncertain journey leaving behind their dead and earthly possessions. The massacre of Mirpur a bustling trade centre and historic walled city of Jammu and Kashmir now in Pak Occupied Kashmir on 25th of Nov. 1947 was the worst massacre of Indian history. As the offer of accession by Maharaja was accepted by Govt of India on 26th of Oct. 1947 after India and Pakistan gained independence, the ill fated Hindu and Sikh minorities living Muslim majority western areas of Jammu region and in Kashmir valley were waiting their Dooms day. The decision of accession of J&K with India and its completed merger with India as its integral part was celebrated like Diwali in Mirpur with lighting of candles and bursting of crackers.

Soon after the independence, Pakistan conceived a military plan to attack Jammu and Kashmir. Code named operation Gulmarg .Pashtun tribes Lashkars from Dir and Waziristan areas were roped in under the direct command of Pak army code and soon armed attacks and looting started in early Sept. in Poonch and Kotli area, about 400 looters entered on 2nd and 3rd Sept, followed by Pak regular army and ex army men. The town of Bhimbar fell at the same time when Indian troops were air lifted of Srinagar on 27th of Oct. 1947. The population of the town swelled to25, 000 souls including migrants from Punjab; it became the boundary line between India and Pakistan on the western side of Jammu and Kashmir State. Pakistan connived with Pakhtoon and attacked Mirpur in full force with the intention of grabbing the whole of Jammu and Kashmir State. But the Mirpur unitedly stood against the invaders to .On the 4th of Nov. 1947, heavy enforcements of the Pakistan Army took position on the ridge known as Palan-Da- Galla and also started heavy firing and tried to besiege the small garrison of State Forces on the river Jhelum about 10 miles from Mirpur city. Under heavy odds, the State Forces decided to retreat falling back to the city. This brought the enemy right to the gates of Mirpur city which now looked within its easy reach. But the people of Mirpur were not prepared to give -in without fighting in collaboration with the small State Force. They organized the defense of the town. Together they repulsed the enemy attack with heavy losses on November 6, 10 and 11, 1947.The morale of the State Garrison got a big boost when on Nov. 12, and the Indian Air Force effectively bombed and strafed the enemy positions around Mirpur city. The Planes appeared in the skies over Mirpur again on November 14 dropping some small arms. Having been loosely packed these was damaged and Pakistan army started using modern weapons and artillery to break the walls of town. There were no supply as the town was already cut off by the fall of Bhimbar in October itself; the only hope was the air dropping of supplies of food and ammunition by air till the reinforcements of Indian army reach to push away the enemy. Frantic massages were sent to Jammu over the wireless by Maharaja Forces to Jammu but in vain. Many of the forceful attacks of the enemy were repulsed. A major attack was carried out by the enemy on 23rd of Nov 1947 from the main eastern gate and was repulsed by Mirpuri youths in hand to hand fight. In a bad luck the only wireless equipment with the state forces broke down and the fresh stronger attack by the enemy forces on 24th morning frightened the state forces that left the battle scene with the information to the civil population to move to safer places. The ensuing fierce fighting throughout the next night put the enemy at bay till morning when they broke the western gate of the city next morning by using heavy artillery. The blood thirsty Pak army and tribal entered the city around 8 a.m. in the morning. Under chaos and confusion people ran around terrified and the city was set on fire by the invaders. Soon poison was distributed to the women to end their lives and not to fall into the hands of enemy. Many who didn't get the poison were done to deaths with swords by their fathers and bothers. The dance of death continued till afternoon and at the end of day 18000 people were slaughtered in most barbaric way of the human history by Pak army and tribal. Five thousand people most of them women and children were taken hostages and taken to Alibeg Gurudawara Sahib which was converted to a concentration camp. Only 2000 people could reach Janger on foot and then escorted by Indian army to Jammu refugee camp. The hapless women and young girls abducted went thorough worst kind violence. The whole of Mirpur was latter dugout to loot the wealth worth billions of Rupees beside gold and silver. The other towns of Jammu province as Rajouri fell on 10th of Nov. where the populations had swelled from 6000 to 11000 with the influx of refugees from the adjoining villages. Most of population was done to death.

The sacrifices of people of Mirpur delayed the enemy for a month till the besieged Poonch was freed and a vital link of Poonch to Jammu was saved from falling into the hands of Pakistan. On this day 25th November Mirpur Balidan Divas is observed

CHAPTER FORTY

BRIGADIER RAJINDER SINGH JAMWAL

Brigadier Rajinder Singh Jamwal

In the face of Pakistani tribal invasion of Jammu and Kashmir Maharaja Hari Singh acceded to India on 26th October 1947 .The date, 26 October, does not stir anything significant in the minds and hearts of the majority of this country. It is not a special birthday or a religious holiday that is etched in the conscience of India. On this day 71 years ago Maharaja Hari Singh of Jammu and Kashmir signed the Instrument of Accession to India as the region was under siege from Pakistani forces. The accord mobilized the Indian Army to repel the invaders weeks after the nation gained Independence and Brigadier Rajinder Singh and his band of warriors who died defending the Kashmir valley. He was martyred the same day Maharaja

Hari Singh signed that historic document uniting Jammu and Kashmir with India, a sacrifice that honored the simple words of that contract. Brigadier Singh was the first recipient of the Mahavir Chakra in Independent India, yet this warrior is barely known to the nation he served, let alone outside the Jammu region. On 21 October 1947, Pakistani forces tried to take control of the region by force, hoping that the dominant Muslim community would support them. They entered Kashmir via Baramulla and targeted the Sikh and Kashmiri Pandits, committing rape and murder .Under siege, on 22 October 1947, Maharaja Hari Singh ordered Brigadier Singh, who served as the chief of army staff of Jammu and Kashmir, to defend the state till the last man and the last bullet. Brig Rajinder Singh was given an order by Maharaja Hari Singh and he just saluted and walked away. Brigadier Singh gathered 110 soldiers and moved to Muzfarabad to counter the invading force of over 6,000 militiamen. He used guerrilla tactics to delay their advance, blowing up the Uri Bridge and stalling them in Mahura and Rampur, inflicting heavy casualties. For four days, Brigadier Singh and his brave jawans hindered the progress of the Pakistani invaders. This may have been the first time in contemporary military history where an army chief personally led soldiers in combat. As Brigadier Singh and his men fought, on 26 October, Maharaja Hari Singh signed the Instrument of Accession joining the Union of India. The Indian military rushed in to back Brigadier Singh; however, just hours away from his position, he was ambushed at Buniyar and fatally wounded. He had held fort and repelled the invaders long enough for the Indian Army to push them back, saving thousands from a brutal onslaught. He carried out his orders to the letter, setting an unparalleled example of courage and patriotism. Brig Rajinder Singh had not stopped the Pakistani invaders, if he had not sacrifice his life Kashmir may not have been a part of India

CHAPTER FORTY-ONE

MAJOR BROWN (OCCUPATION OF GILGIT-BALTISTAN)

Major Brown (Occupation of Gilgit-Baltistan by Pakistan)

In 1935, the Gilgit agency was leased for 60 years by the British from the Maharaja of Jammu and Kashmir because of its strategic location on the northern borders of British India. It was administered by the political department in Delhi through a British officer. The region's security was the responsibility of a military force called the Gilgit Scouts, which was officered by the British .When Lord Mountbatten announced the Transfer of Power in India on June 3, 1947, it was also announced that all treaties and engagements with the princely states of India would also come to an end meaning that all the princely states would achieve their legal independence with the departure of the British on August 15, 1947. Since this announcement meant that the Gilgit Wazarat lease would also lapse, Lord Mountbatten returned the Gilgit Wazarat back to the Kashmir Durbar on August 1, 1947.On August 1, 1947 Maharaja of J&K and Lt. Col. Roger Bacon, the British political agent, handed over the area to Brig. Ghansara Singh, the state's new governor. Hence on August 15, 1947 several legal entities in the region of the State of Jammu and Kashmir, the State of Hunza, the State of Nagar and the tribal territories of Chilas, Koh Ghizr, Ishkoman and Yasin, all achieved their independence. But right at beginning Pakistan attacked Jammu and Kashmir and occupied a major portion of the territory of J&K. The State of Jammu and Kashmir comprised of Jammu, Kashmir, Laddakh, Pakistan Occupied J&K and Gilgit-Baltistan. Under attack from Pakistan and tribal forces the Maharaja of Kashmir decided to throw in his lot with India on October 26, 1947, and an Instrument of Accession was signed. Major Brown, who was Commandant of the Gilgit Scouts, devised a plan under which he secured the accession of Hunza and Nagar states, and the tribal areas, and between the night of October 31 and November 1, 1947 led the Gilgit Wazarat to revolt against the Kashmir Durbar. Then in quick succession, Major Brown arrested the Kashmir appointed Governor, Brigadier Ghansara Singh neutralized the state forces at Bunji, and secured the treasury. On November 2, Major Brown officially raised the Pakistani flag at his headquarters. Two weeks later, a nominee of the Pakistan government, Sardar Mohammed Alam, was appointed the Political Agent, and took possession of the territory. Pakistani army soldiers and tribal's used it as a base to launch attacks on the other towns and cities of the region like Skardu, Dras, Kargil and Leh. But as .The British decision was influenced by their understanding of the reactions of the Arab nations with regard to formation of Pakistan. The British did not want to antagonize the oil-rich nations by apparently taking an anti-Muslim stand at a time when the fears of Soviet communism dominated the West. Major Brown defected on November 1 and the Pakistani forces occupied Gilgit-Baltistan on November 4. Since then, Gilgit-Baltistan has been under Pakistan's administrative control. According to V.P. Menon, secretary of state and Sardar Patel's points man in the integration of states, Kashmir did not have the resources, including financial, to hold Gilgit which was cut off from Srinagar during winters, but the fact remains that no sooner was Gilgit handed over to the maharaja than it came under the mercy of Pakistan. The British officers of Gilgit Scouts: Major William Alexander Brown and Capt. A.S. Mathieson still served Hari Singh as contract officers, though they continued to receive instructions from the political agent for Khyber based in Peshawar which was now Pakistan. As the new governor occupied his official residence in the grandeur of impotence, it was Brown and Mathieson who held the keys to power in Gilgit.Lt Col. Bacon, on transfer from Gilgit was given the Khyber post. This ensured perfect coordination between the Gilgit Scouts and Peshawar. According to the bulletin of Military Historical Society of Great Britain, the broad post-Partition plan had been discussed by Brown and Bacon in June 1947. And after Mathieson arrived in Gilgit, as second in command, the two British officers refined contingency measures, should the maharaja take his state over to India. In such a situation, delivering Gilgit to Pakistan was fairly straightforward. This was accomplished on the night of October 31, 1947. As soon as Maharaja Hari Singh acceded to India, Brown got the Gilgit Scouts to surround the residency and, after a short gun battle, he imprisoned Governor Ghansara Singh. Brown then informed Peshawar about the accession of Gilgit to Pakistan. On November 2, the major raised the Pakistani flag at his headquarters and informed the force that they now served the government in Karachi. Brown and Mathieson had surreptitiously opted for service in Pakistan when the maharaja signed the Instrument of Accession in favour of India. Since Gilgit by this act had become a part of India. The actions of Brown and Mathieson were suspect politically and Brown was certainly acting as a party to a British conspiracy. However, there existed a small number of British soldiers and officials who, in a private capacity as friends of Pakistan, encouraged Brown and Mathieson to be in Gilgit on the eve of the transfer of power. Throughout the Kashmir War (October 22, 1947 to January 1, 1949), Britain successfully ensured that Pakistan's occupation of this region was not disturbed. After Mountbatten's mediatory role and the collapse of the direct talks between Jawaharlal Nehru and Liaquat Ali Khan, the Indian Cabinet planned a full-scale war. But Mountbatten made a monumental blunder of suggesting to Nehru that the UN would promptly direct Pakistan to withdraw the raiders, which would make war unnecessary and Nehru believed him, internationalizing Kashmir in the process.

CHAPTER FORTY-TWO

SAVIOR OF KASHMIR MAQBOL SHERWANI

Savior of Kashmir Maqbol Sherwani

Every year on its Infantry Day the Indian Army commemorates savior of Kashmir Mohd Maqbol Sherwani. It has also constructed a Memorial Hall in his name in Baramulla town. But that is all. None else observes a day for this savior whom the tribal's captured on November 7, 1947 and virtually crucified .A civilian 19-year-old unsung hero, who laid down his life in 1947. Very few people outside Baramulla do know about Mohd Maqbol Sherwani, how he died and what decisive role he played in saving Srinagar from falling to raiders / Pakistani raiders who attacked Kashmir. Sherwani was a boy of 19 who single-handedly thwarted the advance of thousands of raiders (Kabailis) from Baramulla, thereby giving some lead time to the Indian Army to land in Srinagar. He went around on his bike telling the Kabailis, who stormed Baramulla on October 22, 1947, not to advance towards Srinagar as the Indian Army had reached the outskirts of Baramulla. His bluff worked. The enemy froze in its tracks for four days. By then army landed in Srinagar, on October 27 now celebrated as Infantry Day. It has also constructed a Memorial Hall in his name in Baramulla town. But that is all. None else observes a day for this savior whom the tribal's captured on November 7, 1947. He was put on a wooden cross, nailed and fired upon 10-15 times. He remained like that for three days. His body was brought down when the Indian Army reached Baramulla. The Pakistan sponsored tribal's virtually knocking on the gates of Srinagar, the only way to plant Indian boots on the ground was to provide an immediate air bridge to the valley. What followed was an extraordinary airlift hastily organized seemingly from nowhere and speaks volumes not only for the team and staff work between the Air Force and the Army, but also with the Civil Aviation. He was martyred before he could marry Zeba with whom he was engaged. When Mohammad Ali Jinnah visited Kashmir and spoke at Baramulla on his two-nation theory Sherwani forced him to come down from the platform and this stopped his speech.

CHAPTER FORTY-THREE

WOMEN SELF DEFENCE CORPS

Women's self defense Corps

In rare act of bravery and courage Kashmiri Women in particular Kashmiri Pandit women took up arms to defend the mother land from tribal invasion in 1947 and formed women's self defense Corps .Seventy years ago in autumn, the parks and open spaces of the Kashmiri capital Srinagar were taken over by groups of women who practiced military-style drilling and learned how to fire rifles. These were members of Kashmir's women's militia, hastily recruited at the initiative of left-wingers in the face of an invading force which imperiled the city. There was next-to-no military tradition in Kashmir and the sight of Kashmiri women bearing arms was, for many, arresting and startling. It was a moment of political empowerment just at the eruption of the still unresolved Kashmir conflict, so often seen as a territorial contest between India and Pakistan. The women's section of the militia, or the Women's Self Defense Corps as it was known, was established when the threat to Srinagar was still acute. Stories circulated perhaps exaggerated, but with a basis in fact that the tribal forces had raped and abducted women, particularly non-Muslims, as they advanced eastwards along the Jhelum river. The idea behind the militia was that the women of Srinagar would be able to defend their honor should the city be overrun.

The convening of the militia, as with so much of the popular mobilization in support of Sheikh Abdullah, was largely overseen by the small band of communists in Kashmir and their supporters. It seems only to have mustered in Srinagar and probably to have consisted of under a hundred women, many of them teenagers. The recruits were from all communities, but large portion of them belonged small Kashmiri-speaking Hindu minority who made up the larger part of the professions and liberal intelligentsia in Srinagar and Gujjar community .Among their number was Zuni Gujjari, a Muslim woman from a non-privileged background who was a renowned activist in the National Conference, the progressive nationalist party led by Sheikh Abdullah. Her likeness appeared on the cover of the National Conference's 1944 manifesto, New Kashmir, as well as on Kashmir Defends Democracy, a propaganda pamphlet produced in 1948 in support of Sheikh Abdullah and Kashmir's accession to India. According to Krishna Misri who later enrolled in the women's militia the women leaders took charge and gave a new direction to the struggle. However the leaders addressed no controversial woman specific issues for they did not want to come across as social rebels

The immediate threat to Srinagar was lifted within a matter of weeks, though the first Kashmir war between India and Pakistan continued until the close of 1948. The women's militia never saw active service, but it continued to drill and train in the use of firearms, with an Indian army instructor, well into 1948. Those who gained proficiency in shooting were awarded a bag of salt, a commodity then in short supply. The public display of Kashmiri women carrying rifles did not want to come across as social rebels. A contingent of militia members was inspected by Nehru, India's prime minister, when he visited the Kashmir Valley. Members also sought to help some of the tens of thousands of refugees displaced by fighting across the former princely state. By the close of 1948, the women's militia had been disbanded and the much larger men's militia was eventually incorporated into India's armed forces. The communists urged Sheikh Abdullah, once he became Kashmir's prime minister (the only Indian state then to have such a designation), to turn the volunteers into a people's militia. Instead, he restructured men militia in to the force and disbanded so as to marginalize the influence of the left, whose support he no longer needed once in power. Several former members of the women's militia speak warmly of a moment of empowerment for Kashmiri women and regret that the window closed so quickly. The one lasting influence has been on women's education. Sheikh Abdullah set up a Government College for Women in Srinagar, in a building which once housed the widows of the princely family. Several of the women active in the militia taught there and served as the college principal. The popular political mobilization of which the women's militia was part has been largely written out of the competing historical narratives in Kashmir. India, which continues to grapple with a separatist insurgency, does not wish to dwell on Kashmir's arming themselves; Pakistan doesn't want to be reminded of a time when Kashmiri mustered in support of Indian rule; and Kashmiri separatists, many now advocates of independence, are uncomfortable being reminded that seventy years ago Kashmiri took to the streets and parade grounds to support accession to India.

CHAPTER FORTY-FOUR

SHEIKH MOHAMMAD ABDULLAH

Sheikh Mohammad Abdullah

Sheikh Mohammad Abdullah was one of the famous leaders of modern India. Was born December 5, 1905, Soura near Srinagar he died on September 8, 1982. He was educated at the Prince of Wales College (Jammu) and the Islamia College (Lahore now in Pakistan) and received a master's degree in physics from Aligarh Muslim University in 1930 .He was not only the most dominating political figure of modern Jammu & Kashmir State, but he played a significant role in shaping the post-1947 sub-continental politics. He was the most enigmatic and one among the complex leaders ever produced by the state. By the formation of Muslim Conference it was not only Abdullah's fame which multiplied but his thinking also began to grow mature at even faster pace. In his first address to the Conference, he besides other things emphasized on three main issues. Firstly he called on Muslims to unite and to end all sectarian strife. Secondly Abdullah firmly believed that socio-economic and political lot of Kashmiri masses could not be improved unless there is a qualitative Structural Change within government if not its complete end. Undoubtedly, in his formative phase he had relied much on Punjabi Muslim Organizations and Public opinion and used Islamic institutions and symbols to create a mass base and pressure on the state. Sheikh Abdullah after some time he switched on to use economic and other non-religious issues to propagate his political philosophy. He also distanced himself from the Punjabi Muslim organizations once he realized that these were turning more communal .Muslim Conference and under the leadership of Sheikh Mohammad Abdullah reached to its next and very crucial stage in 1939 when the movement was reoriented to give it secular sense so that all sections of the Kashmir could be accommodated irrespective of their religious and sectarian affiliations. Sheikh Abdulla in a statement said communal politics does not suit the temperature of the people of this state and renamed it as National conference. He said communal politics cannot help us in removing the evils of poverty, hunger, illiteracy and above all over slavery. Role in Quit Kashmir Movement The movement launched by the National Conference in May 1946 launched Quit Kashmir moment but it could not receive as much support as was expected by Sheikh Abdulla and his colleagues. Abdulla reiterated in Srinagar the demand that the princely order should quit the state is a logical extension of the policy of quit India. He also maintained that the dynasty has no right; its future should be decided by the people. He called today the people of Kashmir could not be appeased with only a representative system of governance. They want total freedom from the autocratic rule. In May 1946, he was sentenced to nine years in prison for having led the seditious quit Kashmir movement against the Maharaja regime

Sheikh Abdullah as emergency administrator

Sheikh Abdullah as was essentially socialist rather communal aspiration who would have preferred independence for his state had it been possible or falling to it, or retain it as a semi-independent identity under the protection of Nehru's India. However when tribesmen from Pakistan invaded Jammu and Kashmir beginning on October 22, 1947, Maharaja Hari Singh requested military assistance from the government of India. Pakistani government troops provide support for the Pashtun tribesmen 1947. Maharaja Hari Singh signed the Instrument of Accession with the Indian government on October 26, 1947, and Indian troops entered Jammu and Kashmir on October 27, 1947. Sheikh Mohammed Abdullah was appointed as Emergency Administrator of the state of Jammu and Kashmir by Maharaja Hari Singh on October 30, 1947. The tribal's thundering towards Srinagar shouting slogans against the National Conference and creating panic in its rank and file, it became a case of India or death of Sheikh Abdulla. . It was against this backdrop that Sheikh Abdullah provided his fullest support to the accession offer made by the Maharaja of Kashmir, Hari Singh, to the India. As Head of Emergency Administration & Prime Minister of State On 30th October 1947 after signing the instrument of accession, Maharaja Hari Singh by the wishes of the government of India, appointed Sheikh Mohammad Abdullah once his fiercest enemy, as Head of Emergency Administration to work with his own Prime Minister Dewan Mehar Chand Mahajan. There was no clear demarcation of the powers between the two Mahajan and Abdullah. However, Abdullah soon overshadowed the administration because he derived his real powers from popular support, compulsions of the political situation and by the backing of Jawaharlal Nehru. Whereas as Prime Minister Mehar Chand Mahajan was backed by Maharaja Hari Singh whose own position had turned very weak after the tribal invasion. Satisfied with his role New Delhi decided to mark an end to the dual administration and accordingly on 5 March 1948 Sheikh Abdullah was nominated to the office of Prime Minister and was made all set to control the full authority of the state administration. Accordingly, the Emergency Council was converted into a regular council of ministers

Creation of Salamati Fauj and Women's Self Defense Corps

When sheikh Abdullah took charge as emergency administrator. The Jhelum Valley Cart Road was blocked and postal, telegraph and banking services collapsed. Food and fuel, previously imported from West Punjab, was embargoed. Cooking oil and rock salt vanished from the market overnight and prices shot up, creating great hardships for the people. The enthusiasm with which some who favored Pakistan, had received the Kabailis as their agents of deliverance from the Dogra Raj, soon turned to horrified disgust. They found themselves being roughly prodded by their co-religionists to part with their women and anything of value. Dread full stories of the fate of Sikhs and Hindus at Muzfarabad and Uri, and the killings of the nuns at the missionary hospital in Baramulla, quickly reached Srinagar and magnified the all-pervading sense of dread. The officers of Dogra regime had abandoned the police stations and administrative control evaporated in Srinagar. The vacuum created the possibility of igniting inter-community rivalries especially as refugees started staggering into the city from the border areas of the state. Their tales of woe and sufferings roused passions and created great tensions in Srinagar. Rice had vanished from the shops although Sheikh Abdullah's call of Hindu Muslim-Sikh amity had united the people; things were not entirely under his control. There were several zealously Muslim areas in Srinagar and in the rural parts of Kashmir, where people associated with Pakistan. However, Abdullah's overwhelming influence, and the dread of the Kabailis who rapidly became the target of intense hatred prevented any outbreak of communal violence in the city. Sheikh Abdullah called for raising a Salamati Fauj (Peace Army) for the defense of Srinagar at a huge rally he urged people to maintain communal harmony at all costs and to fight the invaders. The Kashmiri responded heartily. The following slogan resonated throughout the city. Sher-i-Kashmir Ka Kya Irshad? (What does the Lion of Kashmir say?) Hindu, Muslim, Sikh Ethihad. (Hindu, Muslim, Sikh Unity.) Exactly when the group was raised the Kabailis swept down from Muzfarabad. Sheikh Abdullah who had been along with his national conference had active support of CPI cadres for his campaign against Hari Singh. Like him the Communists were opposed to Kashmir's union with Pakistan because they knew that such a union would not offer any space for their ideology in an Islamic society. But also had great followers like Maqbol Sherwani who played great role in saving the Kashmir decisive role he played in saving Srinagar from falling to raiders / Pakistani raiders who attacked Kashmir. He went around on his bike telling the Kabailis, who stormed Baramulla on October 22, 1947, not to advance Sherwani was a boy of 19 who single-handedly thwarted the advance of thousands of raiders Kabailis towards

Srinagar as the Indian Army had reached the outskirts of Baramulla. His bluff worked. The enemy froze in its tracks for four days. Who was captured by tribal's captured on November 7, 1947. He was put on a wooden cross, nailed and fired upon 10-15 times. He remained like that for three days. His body was brought down when the Indian Army reached Baramulla. There many other people who played very significant role as emergency officer like Pt. Swoop Nath Saraf who belonged to minority community of Shopian. He belonged to a generation of Kashmiri, who were deeply influenced by world occurrences, especially the Russian revolution. He was as appointed as emergency administrative officer by Sheikh Abdullah. Like a true leader that he discharged his duties effectively and not a single untoward incident under his jurisdiction. It was he who led the popular agitation which continued for nonstop six month (longest post independence era) in 1979 for giving Shopian the much-aspired District status. Putting his full confidence on his national conference cadre and CPI activists Sheikh Abdullah created Salamati Fauj which was a mostly collection of National Conference workers and any able bodied young man who chose to volunteer. Most volunteered spontaneously to guard their Mohalla and properties, to burnish their manly credentials and also to gain some recognition. Guarding against the Kabailis may have been the main motive but joining the Salamati Fauj was also for the ambitious a way to secure a spot in the Emergency administration. The times were desperate, the situation in Srinagar was precarious, and the Kabailis were at the doorstep. Young men patrolled neighborhood and streets guarding banks, post offices and bridges. They only had wooden rifles or stout staffs, but they drilled enthusiastically at Pratap Chowk, which was re-named Lal Chowk (Red Square) after the Red Square in Moscow by Sheikh Abdullah. This renaming and the National Conference's red flag with the insignia of a white plough resembled the Soviet communist's red flag with a hammer and sickle. To the thoughtful observer and for the communists, this was a great victory as it symbolically indicated Sheikh Abdullah's strong inclination with communist ideology. The white plough represented the tenant peasants who would become landowners, once land reforms were enacted. The marching and sloganeering was in revolutionary fervor, and aimed at bolstering the confidence of the people. Each Mohalla had about two dozen volunteers. There no must have been about 10,000 volunteers, but they were woefully lacking in military training or discipline. A formal command structure did not exist, but the Illaqa committees coordinated local gatherings. There was a lot of confusion about who was who, and who really was in charge. There were no uniforms, shoes or weapons, save several musty single-shot rifles and pellet guns used to shoot pigeons until the Indian Army started supplying modern rifles and training the volunteers. They remained untested, because the Indian Army arrived in the nick of time. The Salamati Fauj was subsequently attached to the army, and termed the National Militia. It acted in a support role. Some college students volunteered as guides for the army, which had no knowledge of the Kashmiri language or of the terrain. Another remarkable development was the formation of the Women's Self-Defense Corps (WSDC). This was a radical idea for the conservative Kashmiri society. The Kabailis bogey had created such dread that the idea of self-defense for women, especially unmarried women, rapidly gained ground. The fate of women and girls became a significant part of each family's survival calculus. The convening of the militia, as with so much of the popular mobilization in support of Sheikh Abdullah, was largely overseen by the small band of communists in Kashmir and their supporters. It seems only to have mustered in Srinagar and probably to have consisted of under a hundred women, many of them teenagers. The recruits were from all communities, but large portion of them belonged small Kashmiri-speaking Hindu minority who made up the larger part of the professions and liberal intelligentsia in Srinagar and Gujjar community .Among their number was Zuni Gujjari, a Muslim woman from a non-privileged background who was a renowned activist in the National Conference, the progressive nationalist party led by Sheikh Abdullah. Her likeness appeared on the cover of the National Conference's 1944 manifesto, New Kashmir, as well as on Kashmir Defends Democracy, a propaganda pamphlet produced in 1948 in support of Sheikh Abdullah and Kashmir's accession to India. The immediate threat to Srinagar was lifted within a matter of weeks, though the first Kashmir war between India and Pakistan continued until the close of 1948. The women's militia never saw active service, but it continued to drill and train in the use of firearms, with an Indian army instructor, well into 1948. Those who gained proficiency in shooting were awarded a bag of salt, a commodity then in short supply. . A contingent of militia members was inspected by Nehru, India's prime minister, when he visited the Kashmir Valley. Members also sought to help some of the tens of thousands of refugees displaced by fighting across the former princely state. By the close of 1948, the women's militia had been disbanded and the much larger men's militia was eventually incorporated into India's armed forces. The communists urged Sheikh Abdullah, once he became Kashmir's prime minister (the only Indian state then to have such a designation), to turn the volunteers into a people's militia. Instead, he restructured men militia in to the force and disbanded so as to marginalize the influence of the left, whose support he no longer needed once in power.

CHAPTER FORTY-FIVE

PREM NATH DOGRA

Prem Nath Dogra

Prem Nath Dogra was a leader from Jammu and Kashmir who worked for total integration of the state with India. He was also known as Sher -e –Duggar .Pandit Prem Nath Dogra was a great patriot and had unflinching faith in the country's unity and was opposed to any kind of division or differential treatment to Kashmir. He was opposed to Article 370 .He was instrumental in forming the Praia Parishad party in 1947 along with Balraj Madhok and opposed the policies of Sheikh Abdullah. He was later elected the president of Bharatiya Jana Sangh in 1955 for a brief period. He formed Praja Parishad party in 1947 along with Balraj Madhok and opposed policies of Sheikh Abdullah. Pt. Prem Nath Dogra emerged on the horizon of political scene and challenged the non secular policies of the NC Government. The agitation paralyzed the administration of the state and dead locked further progress and development. Jan Sang president Dr. Shyama Prasad Mukherjee came forward to patronize the agitation started by Pandit Prem Nath Dogra under the under of Praja Parishad. Dr. Shyama Prasad Mukherjee entered into the state with procession by violating permit system issued by the state for terminating the Permit Raj System.

Agitation for abolition of permit system (Ek Vidhan, Ek Nishan, Ek Pradhan)

I

n early 1949, the Praja Parishad started protesting against the policies of the National Conference government led by Sheikh Abdullah. It accused Sheikh Abdullah of trying to Islamize the administration. The Sheikh had broken up the Hindu-majority district of Udhampur and closed down the Sanskrit Research Department. The land and other property of the charitable trust for the upkeep of temples and Sanskrit pathshalas (schools) had been expropriated and the rehabilitation of Hindu and Sikh refugees from Pakistan-held areas was opposed. The study of Urdu was made compulsory for all. The unceremonious dismissal of the Maharaja Hari Singh, had further embittered them and Yuvraj (Prince) Karan Singh's decision to become the first Regent of the State was strongly criticized as a traitorous act legitimizing the Sheikh's actions and as tantamount to selling the Dogras out to the Kashmiris.The government swiftly suppressed it by arresting as many as 294 members of the Praja Parishad including Prem Nath Dogra its president. The Praja Parishad's call for full integration directly clashed with the demands of National Conference for complete autonomy of the state. The Praja Parishad initially contested 28 out of 30 seats allocated to Jammu in the 1951 elections. However, the nomination papers of thirteen of its candidates were rejected on the grounds of technicalities. Sensing that the elections were being railroaded by the ruling National Conference, the Praja Parishad announced a boycott of the elections shortly before the polling. Consequently, all National Conference candidates were declared as winners from the Jammu province. Thus obstructed from democratic participation, the Praja Parishad took to the streets organizing protests. Calling for full integration of the state with the rest of India, the Parishad issued a rallying cry of Ek Vidhan, Ek Nishan, Ek Pradhan (one constitution, one flag and one premier). This was in marked opposition to the state trying to formulate its own constitution, carrying its own flag and calling its head of executive Prime Minister .On 15 January 1952, students staged a demonstration against the hoisting of the state flag alongside the Indian Union flag. They were penalized, giving rise to a big procession on 8 February. The military was called out and a 72-hour curfew imposed. N. Gopalaswami Ayyangar, the Cabinet minister in charge of Kashmir affairs, came down to broker peace, which was resented by Sheikh Abdullah. By this time, the Bharatiya Jana Sangh was formed in Delhi to champion nationalist politics, and the Praja Parishad became its affiliate in Jammu and Kashmir. Even though Jana Sangh won only 3 seats in the Indian Parliament in the 1951–52 general elections, Shyama Prasad Mukherjee was a powerful leader commanding a big block of support from various opposition parties. The Party and Mukherjee took up the cause of Jammu with vigor. The Praja Parishad submitted a memorandum to the President of India in June 1952, calling for full integration and staged a big demonstration outside the Indian Parliament. The Hindu Mahasabha Member of Parliament N. C. Chatterjee ridiculed the autonomy of Jammu and Kashmir as a Republic within a Republic .In order to break the constitutional deadlock; the National Conference was invited to send a delegation to Delhi. The 1952 Delhi Agreement was formulated to settle the extent of applicability of the Indian Constitution to the state. Following this the Constituent Assembly abolished the monarchy in Kashmir, and adopted an elected Head of State (Sadr-i Riyasat). However, the Assembly was slow to implement the remaining measures agreed in the Delhi Agreement. The Praja Parishad undertook a civil disobedience campaign for a third time in November 1952, which again led to repression by the state government. The Parishad's had eight-point program demanded the abrogation of Article 370; full integration of the State into the Indian Union; full application of the Indian Constitution; removal of the distinction between state-subjects and Indian citizens; complete jurisdiction of the Supreme Court; removal of customs barriers between Kashmir and India; fresh elections to the Kashmir Constituent Assembly; and investigation of corruption in the State administration by an impartial tribunal and complete merger of the sate into main land India. Jammu reverberated with the popular slogan Ek desh mein do Vidhan, do Nishan, do Pradhan, nahi chalega, nahi chalega' (In one country, two constitutions, two flags and two chiefs will not work; will not be tolerated .The Parishad accused Abdullah of communalism (sectarianism), favoring the Muslim interests in the state and sacrificing the interests of the others. In May 1953, Shyama Prasad Mukherjee made a bid to enter Jammu and Kashmir, citing his rights as an Indian citizen to visit any part of the country. Abdullah prohibited his entry and promptly arrested him when he attempted. An estimated 10,000 activists were imprisoned in Jammu, Punjab and Delhi, including Members of Parliament. Unfortunately, Mukherjee died in detention on 23 June 1953, leading to an uproar in entire country and precipitating a crisis that spiraled out of control. Sheikh Abdullah lost majority within his five-member Cabinet. He was dismissed from the post of Prime Minister and put in prison, by the orders of Sadr-i Riyasat Karan Singh.Bakshi Ghulam Mohammad, who succeeded Abdullah as the Prime Minister, implemented all the measures of the Delhi Agreement, making further concessions of powers to the Union government. The Praja Parishad agitation largely subsided after these events.

Printed by Libri Plureos GmbH in Hamburg,
Germany